how to enjoy your life in spite of it all

how to

life in spite

enjoy your

of it all

ken keyes, jr.

LIVING LOVE PUBLICATIONS

This book may be obtained through your local bookstore or you may order it from Cornucopia Books, 790 Commercial Ave., Coos Bay, OR 97420, for $4.95 plus $1.25 for postage and handling.

International Standard Book Number: 0-915972-01-8

Copyright 1980 by Living Love Publications

Library of Congress Cataloging in Publication Data

Keyes, Kenneth S.
  How to enjoy your life in spite of it all.

  Includes index.
  1. Conduct of life.   I. Title.
BJ1581.2.K454   158'.1   79-88956
ISBN 0-915972-01-8

First printing, June, 1980	49,000
Second printing, January, 1985	15,000
Total in print	64,000

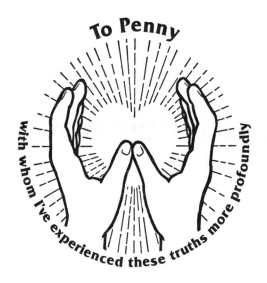

To Penny

with whom I've experienced these truths more profoundly

Acknowledgments

Many, many people have contributed directly or indirectly to this book. Carole Thompson Lentz was the first to give me the benefit of her excellent insights and suggestions. Kris Nevius, G.B. and Char Cornucopia also contributed suggestions from their years of experience both in teaching and applying the Living Love Methods in their daily lives. I feel a love and involvement with Carole, Kris, G.B. and Char that is precious to me.

Lenore Sheets originally transcribed the manuscript from tapes, and Galadriel generously volunteered her help in retyping the entire manuscript in both the first and second revisions. Britta Zetterberg, Maggie Gold and Terilyn Gilliam helped in typing revisions and offering many worthwhile suggestions. Many others freely gave their assistance and support both personally and editorially during the year it took to prepare the manuscript for publication. I especially wish to express my appreciation to Marc Medoff, Dennis Powell, Gary Fisher and Mariah Janus. I also want to acknowledge the useful feedback I received from the seventy-five students at Cornucopia who took a one-week seminar based on the manuscript. Many thanks are due to Harry Klopf for furnishing helpful material.

Sunny Shender produced all the diagrams in the text. Meg Studer created the loving energy drawings. Bunnie Tuffli of Typola handled the typesetting and Kathleen Roberts made the layout. Bill Hannig and Dan Piel offered some excellent suggestions in typographical design.

One of the greatest pleasures in working on this book was the many hours I spent with Penny Hannig with her reading it aloud. The book has greatly benefited from her astute and penetrating insights. We had the fun of playing with the printed words and sentences to help them effectively describe the living experience of applying the Twelve Pathways in one's life. Since the task was an impossible one to begin with, I must ask each reader to compassionately fill in the many lapses and deficiencies in sharing the living science of human happiness in the medium of printed type.

Ken Keyes, Jr.

Santa Cruz, California
January, 1980

Contents

Introduction

I'VE HAD TWO REMARKABLE TEACHers in my life: Dr. William McCall of Teachers College, Columbia, and Alfred Korzybski of the Institute of General Semantics. Each in his own way helped me wonder whether it just might be possible to create a science of happiness—that is, to formulate clear principles that when applied moment to moment enable a person to live a socially contributing and individually happy life. Neither of these teachers furnished me with the answer to this supreme riddle of human life. But each provided me with provocative clues that kept me pondering this puzzle of puzzles. I never found any university courses such as Happiness 101, and the few books that dealt with happiness treated it as an art largely based on folk wisdom. Human happiness seemed to be a hit-and-miss affair—certainly not a workable science based on clear principles with high levels of predictability.

And then it happened. In 1970 when I was 49 years old, I began to discover the missing parts of the jigsaw puzzle I needed to formulate a science of happiness. By 1972 I was able to establish and test in my own life an exact methodology that can enable one to create higher and more stable levels of happiness—depending upon the level of skill in applying it in one's day-to-day stream of consciousness. Since then, hundreds of thousands of people have, in varying degrees, become aware of this methodology.

I refer to this as the Science of Happiness. I also call it the Living Love Way because of **the central part that the experience of love must play in creating a happy life.** (I'm talking about love—not sex!) This is a holistic way of life, encompassing four vital aspects: 1. exercise, 2. nutrition, 3. learning to love more and demand less with the help of the six specific Living Love Methods and finally, 4. using our strength and freedom to love and serve the world.

In this book I am describing only the first of the six Living Love Methods—the Twelve Pathways. These are, however, the core of the system. You will learn how you can use this method in your mind at the moment you are feeling afraid, frustrated, angry, irritated, resentful, bored, worried, jealous or emotionally upset in any way. These methods not only deal effectively with these emotional **symptoms** of unhappiness, but also chip away at the basic **causes** of unhappiness—your haphazard desire systems that create an unworkable experience of self—and of life. Most people's happiness is dependent on the people and environment around them fitting the models in their minds. With the Living Love Way, your happiness no longer depends on the behavior of others. It is primarily dependent on the skill with which you can use the Living Love techniques for operating your mind. This puts all the aces in your hand!

LOVE IS THE ANSWER

As my work in this area enlarged, I found that the late Pitirim A. Sorokin (Professor of Sociology at Harvard University from 1930 to 1964, and President of the American

Sociological Association from 1965 to 1968) during a long
career of studying social relationships stated that the following were confirmed by experimental studies:

Hate begets hate, violence engenders violence, hypocrisy is answered by hypocrisy, war generates war, and
love creates love.

Unselfish love has enormous creative and therapeutic
potentialities, far greater than most people think. Love is
a life-giving force, necessary for physical, mental, and
moral health.

Altruistic persons live longer than egoistic individuals.

Children deprived of love tend to become vitally, moral-
ly, and socially defective.

Love is the most powerful antidote against criminal,
morbid, and suicidal tendencies; against hate, fear, and
psychoneuroses.

It is an indispensable condition for deep and lasting
happiness.

It is goodness and freedom at their loftiest.

It is the finest and most powerful educational force for
the ennoblement of humanity.

Finally, only the power of unbounded love practiced in
regard to *all human beings* can defeat the forces of inter-
human strife, and can prevent the pending extermination
of man by man on this planet. Without love, no armament,
no war, no diplomatic machinations, no coercive police
force, no school education, no economic or political
measures, not even hydrogen bombs can prevent the
pending catastrophe. Only love can accomplish this
miracle, providing, however, we know well the nature of
love and the efficient ways of its production, accumulation, and use.*

We know less about "love energy" than about heat, light,
electricity and other forms of energy. "It is amazing how
little the empirical sciences have to offer on the subject of
love," psychologist A. H. Maslow correctly pointed out.

*Reprinted from *The Ways and Power of Love* by Pitirim A. Sorokin, The
Beacon Press, Boston, Massachusetts, 1954. vii - viii.

"Particularly strange is the silence of the psychologists. Sometimes this is merely sad or irritating, as in the case of the textbooks of psychology and sociology, practically none of which treat the subject . . . . More often the situation becomes completely ludicrous. [As a rule] the word 'love' is not even indexed [in psychological and sociological works]." As psychiatrist Eric Fromm expressed it, "Love is the only sane and satisfactory answer to the problem of human existence." And love has long been an essential part of all spiritual paths; for example, Christ's dictum that we "love one another" and the statement that "God is love."

MY CONTINUING WORK

I began to use the Living Love Way to clean up separate-self functionings of my mind that were making me create dissatisfaction and unhappiness. After ten years of inner work, I seem to have mainly one area of vulnerability left. (This has to do with having training centers in which I offer the highest quality of training I am capable of.) My level of moment-to-moment enjoyment of life has been incredibly increased by using the Living Love techniques of happiness. **The wonderful cumulative effectiveness of these techniques when skillfully and persistently applied over a period of years is delightful and satisfying.**

Based on my own personal experience, I wrote the *Handbook to Higher Consciousness* in 1972, of which there are 770,000 copies in print today. It had practically no advertising. Its sales zoomed because people bought so many copies for their friends.

Our headquarters is at Coos Bay, Oregon, where we offer weekend, one-week and longer programs in applying the Science of Happiness in one's everyday life. It is operated in the spirit of love and service on a nonprofit basis. Tens of thousands of people have now taken Living Love trainings. Occasionally "Opening Up" weekend workshops are also offered in the larger cities throughout the nation. Appendix 2 tells you how to get a schedule of these life-giving trainings.

THE TWELVE PATHWAYS

The Twelve Pathways are a tool that simplifies your applying the Science of Happiness in your life. *How to Enjoy Your Life in Spite of It All* shows you how to apply them moment to moment in your life. This book does not present the entire Living Love system. To round out your knowledge of all of the Living Love Methods and how to use them, you may wish to read the other books listed in Appendix 3.

This book has been written so that you can understand it without prior study. I recommend that you read it at least three times if you are really interested in using it to improve your life. First, read it for intellectual understanding. Next read it again to enlarge your awareness of how it applies to your life. Then read it a third time to permit your mind to create precious insights that deepen both your level of understanding and your knowledge of how to apply it in your life.

When skillfully used, the principles of happiness in this book will help your life work in a way that you may now think is impossible. For this book in the last analysis is not about the Science of Happiness or about Living Love—it is about how your mind operates and how your life operates. It is really about you.

Coos Bay, Oregon   Ken Keyes, Jr.
August, 1984

PART I

The Science of Happiness

Our minds constantly create mental models of how things "should be"—and those thoughts are almost always different from "what is" in our lives. In spite of our lifelong efforts, the changing world we live in seldom fits our desire systems in a cozy, comfortable way. Trying to create a happy experience of life—based only on what we have coinciding with what we want—is like building our houses on quicksand.

1

life is lousy

LET'S START OUT REALISTICALLY by recognizing that life is lousy. And I mean it's really lousy. A lot of the time we don't get what we want. This applies whether we are one year old, in our teens, in our twenties, forties, sixties or any age. Our bodies are often vulnerable to pain and sickness. Rising prices and taxes drag us down. Earning a living is a treadmill. We're choking in environmental pollution. Whether we are walking, driving or flying, our modes of travel constantly threaten to maim, kill or bankrupt us. War and nuclear disaster hang heavy over our heads.

No matter how successful we are, someone is going to eclipse us some day—if not sooner. And our love life—let's not get into that! About half of our marriages end up in divorce. If our children really tried to hurt us, they couldn't do a much better job. And our parents don't really understand us. Money is a constant problem. Everything we own is steadily deteriorating and will eventually be on the junk heap. This also applies to our bodies, which are growing older every day and will inevitably die.

THE EPIDEMIC OF UNHAPPINESS

Life is not only lousy—it's unfair, too. It's just not fair for some people to be healthier, wealthier, prettier, luckier, more talented, intelligent and popular than others.

A lot of the time we don't get what we strongly desire in our lives. Occasionally we are able to fight hard enough to get it. But then we find that, by forcing things, we've set up more problems in our lives and have alienated some people. And even when we get what we want, we then worry about holding onto it. This is so whether it be a lover, money or success. We work hard to get things we think will enable us to live peaceful, happy lives—and we usually aren't fully satisfied even if we happen to get them. Lasting happiness constantly eludes us.

Even if we did manage to be happier than we are, all the misery, unhappiness and death around us would keep pulling us down into sympathetic depressions. We look around us to see if there is anyone else living a happy life. We find that there are a lot of people who maintain an impressive melodrama, but when we really get into the nitty-gritty of their lives, we find that the shoe, although it looks good outside, is pinching inside.

So life is lousy. Let's face it. Is it possible to be really happy? I don't mean to just find occasional pleasure. We all know how to find moments or hours of pleasure. **But can we create an experience of life that is continuously enjoyable? Or largely so?** The lives of most of the people around us seem to indicate that we can't. We live in an epidemic of misery, worry, unsolvable problems and disappointment. Perhaps the most we can expect from our struggling, problem-filled lives is an occasional pleasure break . . . .

OUR ANTIQUATED PROGRAMMING

BUT WAIT. Everything above is based on an outdated separate-self "jungle" type of programming (or set of mental habits) with which we usually operate our minds and our lives. **This book is clearly saying that it doesn't have to be this way.** If you hear its message, you will discover it is possible to retrain your mind so that you can continuously enjoy your life. If you are willing to become a student of the mind, you can discover how it operates to create your experience of unhappiness. You may then begin working on some of your mental habits **in order to transform your experience of your life!**

All of the situations mentioned above (as examples of the hopelessness of finding happiness) can occur in your life—**and you can still enjoy your life.** This book will give you clear information on what you need to do to avoid becoming an "effect" of the above-mentioned situations in your life. **You can become a creative "cause" of your experience. Your life can go up and down—but your experience of happiness does not need to go up and down with it!** You can still be happy regardless of what happens! It takes understanding, determination and lots of practice. But doesn't everything worthwhile require as much?

It is difficult to retrain your mind to do this. But it is not as difficult as living out an unhappy life with all of its anger, fear, jealousy, resentment, irritation, alienation, anxiety, loneliness and boredom. And the beautiful thing about the techniques in this book is that they can help you to create a happy life—even if you think they won't work. They are not based on a belief system any more than hammering a nail into a piece of wood is based on a belief system. Just do it. It works.

Your control over the basic conditions of your life is usually minimal, but your ability and skill in creating your EXPERIENCE of life can be maximal. Therein lies the secret of happiness.

2
accepting the unacceptable

THE MIRACLE OF LEARNING TO enjoy your life no matter what happens does not take place automatically. It requires a lot of continuous attention and determination on your part. So let's get started. We'll begin by redefining two words, so that we may use them as tools for doing this inner work. These words are "addiction" and "preference."

AN ADDICTION IS AN EMOTION-BACKED DE-MAND OR DESIRE FOR SOMETHING YOU TELL YOURSELF YOU MUST HAVE TO BE HAPPY. Addic-

4

tions, or addictive demands, can be on yourself, other people, objects or situations. You can always tell when you have an addiction because:

1. It creates tension in your body.
2. It makes you experience separating emotions, such as resentment, anger, fear, jealousy, worry, anxiety and boredom. Look into your own experience and notice how the above emotions make you feel separate from yourself or others. Separating emotions are contrasted with unifying emotions, which give you experiences of acceptance, love, joy, happiness, peace and purpose in life.
3. Your mind is insistently telling you that things must be different in order for you to enjoy your life here and now.
4. Your mind makes you think there is something important to win or lose in this situation—that your happiness depends on the soap opera.
5. You feel that you have a "problem" in your life—instead of experiencing life as an enjoyable "game" to be played.

Addictions are always the cause of separating emotions. If something triggers one of your addictions, an unpleasant experience will be neurologically activated by your mind. Just as striking a key on a piano may be seen as a cause of the note sounding, triggering an addictive program in your mind will automatically make you create a separating emotional experience such as fear, frustration, irritation or anger.

Your addictive emotion-backed demand is the cause; your emotional response is the effect. You have many, many addictive demands to which your mind and body emotionally respond. You also have the capacity to do something about it so as to increase your level of happiness.

5

PREFERENCES NEVER CAUSE UNHAPPINESS

A preference is a desire that does not make you upset or unhappy if it is not satisfied. Fortunately, most of the programming in your mind is preferential—or you would have had a nervous breakdown by now. Carrying addictions is very hard on the mind and the body; preferences, however, open up your life and let you enjoy whatever happens. Unlike addictions, they do not keep you constantly pushing your emotional emergency alarm buttons. Preferences are the spice of life!

Let's suppose you want to take a long walk after supper tonight. If your mind is addictively demanding to take this walk, you'll automatically make yourself feel deprived and upset if it rains. If your mind has preferential programming to walk after supper, you can enjoy the walk if it doesn't rain, but you will not make yourself upset if it does.

Preferences enable you to flexibly be with whatever life is offering you in the here and now. Upleveling addictions to preferences is the key technique in the Science of Happiness. You might even find you can enjoy walking in the rain. But don't get addicted to it!

PREFERENCES MAKE LIFE EASY

The staff of our training center has written *THE METHODS WORK . . . if you do!** In this excellent "how to do it" book, they indicate that the distinction between an addiction and a preference is in your internal emotional experience. It is not necessarily in your actions, desires, opinions, models or thoughts. When you use preferences, **you emotionally accept** what is happening in your life. You might still put a lot of energy into changing it, but you do not feel attached to the results of your actions. **You**

*You may order THE METHODS WORK . . . if you do! by sending $4.50 plus $1.25 for mailing to Cornucopia Books, 790 Commercial Ave., Coos Bay, OR 97420. This is a workbook that describes and helps you practice all the six Living Love Methods.

emotionally experience that your happiness is not dependent on your desire being met.

When you reprogram or uplevel your addiction to a preference, the following is true:

1. You can dislike "what is."
2. You can try to change "what is."
3. You can hold on to your opinion about what's right
   or fair.
4. BUT, YOU NO LONGER HAVE TO MAKE YOUR-
   SELF UNHAPPY.

There is nothing to create your unhappiness once you
eliminate your addictive demand. You can want things
without jeopardizing your happiness. You can still put energy into trying to change your situation. **You can often
change it much more effectively because you are in a preferential space.** You'll also have more energy to put into
making changes in life situations. You can still have the
opinions you had before. Your models and opinions don't
necessarily change when you uplevel your addiction. **They
just become preferential instead of addictive.** You emotionally **accept** "what is" but that doesn't mean you have
to like it. You can still want it to be different.

Here is an example of the above points using the addictive demand that the clutch on my car not keep slipping.

If I uplevel this addiction to a preference:

1. **I can still not like it when my clutch keeps slipping.**
2. **I can put energy into fixing it.**
3. **I can keep my opinion that the clutch shouldn't be
   slipping.**
4. **I can emotionally accept the fact that the clutch is slipping, and therefore I don't have to make myself unhappy.**

Now here's a word of warning. The above paragraphs
have very carefully defined how we wish to use the word
"preference" so as to make it an effective tool for our inner

work. In spite of this, everyone's mind tries to protect its addictions by creating confusion about preferences. It often tries to tell us that if we just preferred something, people would run over us or ignore us. It tries to tell us that we've got to have the anger generated by addictions to deal effectively with many of life's situations. The rational mind will tell itself that we are absolutely right about a matter— so we must addictively demand or righteously make ourselves upset over whatever we're addicted to.

If you reread this section ("Preferences Make Life Easy"), you may begin to see why the above confusions are based on a misunderstanding of how we're using the term "preference." As you continue reading the balance of this book, your insight can gradually deepen so that you may experience that preferences may actually make you more effective than addictions in getting what you want. This insight is to be supremely valued, for it will enable you to begin the deeper levels of inner work so that you can enjoy your life— in spite of it all.

ADDICTIONS CAUSE SUFFERING

Let's look at the diagram entitled "Addictions Are the Immediate, Practical Cause of Unhappiness." The long box at the bottom represents "what is"—the reality of the here and now in your life. **"What is" represents everything external to the screen of your consciousness.** This includes the entire situation of the world around you, as well as everything people say and do, and the way your mind, emotions and body operate.

Now let's suppose "what is" feeds through one of your addictive filters. If it does not meet the stringent requirements of the addictive programming in your mind, you will automatically trigger separating emotions, such as anger, fear, jealousy and resentment. If, however, "what is" feeds into preferential programming in your mind, **you can enjoy**

ADDICTIONS ARE THE IMMEDIATE, PRACTICAL CAUSE OF UNHAPPINESS

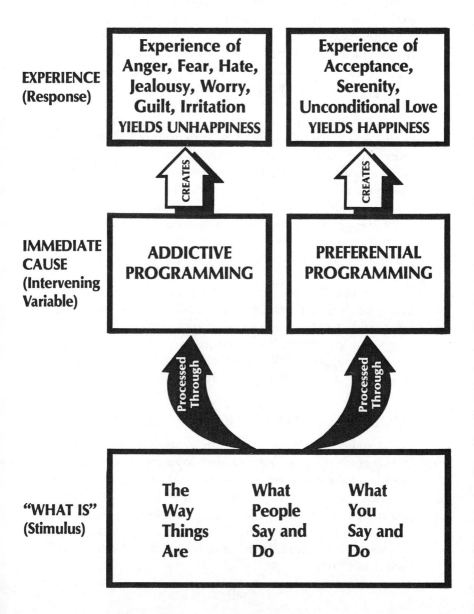

your life whether or not your preference is being met by the here and now of your life.

When you relate this diagram to the operation of your mind, you will understand how addictions make you vulnerable to creating the experience of separateness, alienation, deprivation and unhappiness when "what is" is not fitting the addictive models in your head. **Addictions create separateness and suffering; preferences never do.**

When your addictive emotion-backed demands are being met by the people and situations around you, your mind is not disturbed. On the contrary, your experience can be similar to that which you create with preferential programming. You may even create exhilarating and exciting experiences when life suits your addictive demands. But they keep you vulnerable. It's as though the road you are traveling is booby-trapped with explosive mines just waiting to be stepped on. There is an impish quality about life that constantly pulls you into situations that are absolutely perfect for getting you in touch with your various addictions!

When you live your life with programming that is generally preferential, you can see your life in a humorous light. You can play it as a game. You can make it O.K. to win some and lose some. Your energy can flow to get a lot of things done, since it is not being wasted by addictive turmoil. You can deeply enjoy yourself and your life.

IMMEDIATE AND PRACTICAL CAUSE

Your ability to benefit from the growth that is described in this book requires that you develop a penetrating understanding of the statement "Addictions are the immediate, practical cause of unhappiness." Let's look at the diagram again. There is no direct connection between "what is" and your experience of life. Only your addictive programming connects your anger, fear, hate, jealousy and worry with "what is"!

We blindly assume that "what is" determines our experience. But as we carefully look at our lives, and examine the operation of our minds and emotions, we discover that there is an "intervening variable"—our addictive or preferential programming. Thus addictions are the **immediate** cause of our unhappiness.

Addictions are also the **practical** cause of our unhappiness. And what do we mean by practical? It simply means that we can effectively do something about our addictions. In many life situations, trying to change "what is" in our lives so that it fits our addictive demands is like beating our heads on a brick wall. How often do people say, "Thank you for showing me how dumb, inefficient or wasteful I am— I'll try to do better"? How often have you felt the hopelessness of trying to shape up your parents, spouses, children, friends, bosses or workers so that they won't trigger your emotion-backed demands? Although it's not easy, **the simplest, surest and most practical way** to improve your experience of life is to work on your addictive programming— and not be **entirely dependent on successfully changing "what is" in the world in order for you to be happy.**

Part Six of this book will show you how to use several mental exercises that can gradually increase your skill in upleveling your addictive emotion-backed demands into preferences. In other words, you can use your mind to change the way in which your mind operates so that it will give you more energy, more perceptiveness and insight, more love for yourself and others, more joy and happiness and the experience of purpose in your life.

You can use these mental exercises to play a challenging game with yourself in which you use your life experiences as stepping stones to growth. Since some addictive programmings are lightly held by the ego-mind, you can have the reinforcing experience of upleveling some addictions to preferences rather rapidly. (Please refer to the glossary at the back of this book for unfamiliar terms, such as "egomind.") Thus, some addictions can be made into preferences within the first few weeks after you begin using these methods to work on yourself. Others will take months, and there will be several "snarled" addictive areas that can take years to uplevel to preferences—if then.

Or you may choose not to work on some of the heavier addictive demands now in your mind. You may wish to simply work on taking responsibility for your experience and not blaming others for the fear, anger or resentment that your mind is creating. Even though you have not up-leveled an addiction to a preference, your relationships with other people will improve. You will be consciously aware of the operation of your mind instead of unconsciously running off addictive programming in robot style. Your mind will recover its equilibrium much faster when you trigger an addiction if you are aware of the addictive tapes it is running—and you just accept the fact that that's what's happening. In other words, **you don't have to be addicted to getting rid of your addictions.**

DON'T TAKE THIS LIGHTLY

At this point, you've read a description of how addictions and preferences operate. You've seen the diagram showing the relationship between "what is," your programming and your internal emotional experience. And this probably looks simple to you.

But . . . if you really want to start actually using this in your life, it will mean a virtual revolution in the way you operate your mind! Its far-reaching effects on your feelings, your thoughts, your words and your actions will be as profound as if a factory converted from manufacturing automobiles into making clothing.

To enter into this more effective consciousness, first look at how your mind has been trained to **automatically** connect "what is" with your emotional experience. Notice that the diagram shows no such direct connection. (Please turn to the diagram and see that there is no direct connection between the bottom box and the top boxes.) All your life you have been training your mind to directly associate "what is" with your experience. You've been unaware that your programming is **a totally controlling factor** that operates in between (1) "what is" and (2) the experience you create in your life.

Notice how the false statements below imply that "what is" in our lives causes our internal experience of life:

False Statement	Accurate Statement
"You make me so mad."	"Your actions get me in touch with addictions that trigger anger in me."
"I can't stand that noise."	"My addictive models make me reject that noise."
"My mother's death saddens me."	"I feel sad because I'm addictively demanding that my mother not die."
"I feel awful because I made a mistake."	"When I make a mistake, my addictive self-rejecting programming makes me create the experience of feeling awful."
"My injury from the car accident makes me depressed."	"My addictive demand that I not have been injured in the car accident causes feelings of depression in me."
"Not having sex tonight makes me angry."	"When my addictive demand for sex is unmet, I make myself feel angry."
"Losing money makes me resentful."	"My addictive demand that I not lose money creates the feeling of resentment in me."

This shifting of emphasis from **a sole preoccupation with the factual level ("what is") to our addictive mental habits** is an absolutely essential step toward enjoying our lives more—and often becoming more effective in changing "what is." As we'll discuss in the next chapter, our lives don't work well when we run addictive programming. Unfortunately, our minds hide this faulty operation from us and instead often give us the feeling that we act more effectively when we operate from addictions.

A book can only go so far in helping you understand this shifting of emphasis from outside to inside. You'll have to develop this insight for yourself through consciously working to apply the things we're talking about in the moment-to-moment activity in your mind. Our society, our mental habits, and our language all conspire against us to reinforce the illusion that the way we experience life is based only on what's happening in our lives.

It will not only take insight but also strong determination to break through this illusion and develop a functioning awareness that it is always your programming (addictive or preferential) that is the immediate, practical cause of your experience. In other words, the world hasn't been doing it to you. You've been doing it to yourself!

*B*ecause of our powerful rational
minds, we can tear each other apart,
both individually and collectively,
unless we are guided in our everyday
lives by the heart space. Love is not
only essential to human happiness—it
is essential to human survival. And
it's a lot more fun, too.

3
resisting, clinging and ignoring

L*ET'S SEE HOW ADDICTIONS
and preferences work to create your emotional experience
and also how they determine your level of insight into
what is actually taking place around you in your life. "The
Key to Happiness" diagram on the next page indicates that
addictive demands operate in your mind in three ways:

1. Addictive demands make you **resist** or reject what is
   here and now in your life.
2. Addictive demands make you **cling** or hold on to something or someone. You may create fear by clinging to

THE KEY TO HAPPINESS

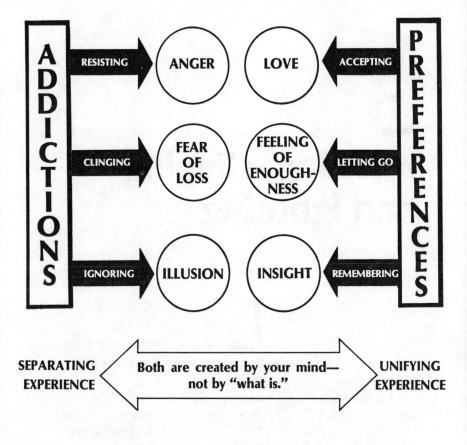

The trick of the ego is to make you feel that your experience is based on "what is" instead of the addictive or preferential programming in your mind.

that which is now a part of your life. Or, as in the case of someone whose "life is ruined" because his/her beloved died, you may create grief by emotionally clinging to that which you formerly had.

3. Addictive demands make you **ignore** actual life facts by blanking out things either from the memory banks of your mind or from the incoming reports of your eyes and ears.

From the diagram, you can see that when your addictive demands make you emotionally **resist** what is here and now in your life, you will be vulnerable to creating the experience of anger—or other power-type emotions, such as irritation and resentment. Always remember that intelligently trying to change "what is" in your life from a preferential space does not "jam up" the operation of your mind. It's the addictive emotion-backed demand that causes all the havoc!

The diagram indicates that when your addictive demands make you **cling,** you will create an experience of fear and insecurity. When your addictive demands make your mind function in a way that **ignores** relevant aspects of a situation, you are trapped in illusions and ignorance.

Now let's look at how the mind operates when it is working from preferential programming. Instead of resisting, preferences enable us to emotionally **accept** what is here and now in our lives. This emotional acceptance of "what is" opens our minds to create the experience of love, inner peace and enjoyment—and at the same time we can play the game of trying to shape up the world to fit our preferential models.

Whereas addictions make us cling, preferential programming enables us to **let go emotionally.** With addictive programming we experience deficiency—that we're not enough or that our lives are not enough. We cling and hold on unwisely and compulsively. On the other hand, preferential programming lets us create the experience of enoughness.

Since we are experientially rich, **we can afford to be generous with ourselves and others.** We can enjoy what we have without neurotically clinging—and worrying about losing it.

Instead of ignoring, preferential programming enables the mind to function in a way that **remembers** or notices relevant aspects of a situation. Our preferences thus enable us to operate with insight, perceptiveness and perspective. They let us have a panoramic view of what's happening instead of being trapped in "tunnel vision." They help us be gentle with ourselves. **Preferences enable us to tune-in to the finest possible integration of what we desire and what's reasonably "gettable" in our here-and-now life situation.** This is called wisdom.

Sometimes the mind can simultaneously resist, cling and ignore in a given situation. For example, if your television is stolen, addictively resisting or rejecting the situation can push your anger button. Addictively clinging to the $600 you paid for it can make you trigger fear and worry. At the same time, your addictions can cause you to ignore how you sometimes set up this situation in your life by forgetting to lock your front door.

On the other hand, when your mind is using preferential programming, you can simultaneously **accept** "what is," **let go** of what's passing and clearly **remember** all of the relevant aspects of each situation. This represents an optimal level of functioning of your nervous system.

"Accepting," "letting go" and "remembering" as used in the diagram refer to the functioning of your mind and how you create your internal emotional experience of life. They do not necessarily limit your choices in action. For example, your mind can function by accepting, letting go and remembering—and on the soap opera level, you can still choose to play the game of calling the police and trying to recover your television set. What you accept is the life fact that the television is not sitting in your living room right now. You can still act freely to do what you want about it. When you let go of the addictive demand in your mind, you create a sense of the enoughness in your life even with this loss. You do not necessarily have to stop trying to recover or replace it. You may choose to play the game of life by holding on tightly—but are always prepared to let go lightly.

THE THREE POISONS

Let's look again at what "The Key to Happiness" diagram is saying. A mind that is disturbed by a muddying stream of addictive emotion-backed demands will be characterized by what Chögyam Trungpa has called "the three poisons"— resisting, clinging and ignoring. The problem with the addictive programmings in your mind is that they make you angry when you resist, fearful when you cling and subject to illusion when you ignore or "forget."

But your addictions are not "bad" in themselves. This is an important point to realize. If you view addictions as "bad," you judge yourself and others for having them. Such criticalness greatly impedes your ability to uplevel addictions to preferences.

Your addictive security, sensation and power (including pride and prestige) demands make you emotionally resist in a way that involves your entire body-mind in trying to push something away. When you see life with perspective, you will notice that **most of the things you addictively resist in your life persist year after year.** Your compulsive emotion-backed demands so limit your freedom of choice that you often miss out on simple, effective opportunities. In other words, emotionally resisting is self-defeating. But at the moments of emotional resistance, that is not your experience of what is happening. You think you are valiantly fending off a real threat that could ruin you.

Your ego-mind constantly tries to enhance its domain. And once ego's territory is increased, your mind is not willing to let go of something that life is taking away from you. You are thus constantly vulnerable to "clinging," that is, emotionally demanding and insisting that what is now in your life not change. You don't realize that the same universe that gave you a possession or a relationship may be waiting to give you something even more beautiful in your life if you will just turn loose of what it previously gave you. But addictions blind you and make you emotionally cling—and you thus set up another cycle of anxiety and misery.

Your addictive demands destroy your deeper potential for enjoying life. Addictions hinder your integration of inside and outside energies by neurologically making you "block out" or ignore things. I'm sure you have noticed how easy it is to forget things when you are addicted. The ego-mind has total control of the operation of the memory banks in the brain. It can make you "forget" facts and information when these would mellow the addictive demand that the mind is running.

Your addictive demands can actually keep you from seeing or hearing what is right before you. They can make you totally misunderstand what a person is clearly telling you. When addictive tension is high within you, the functional intelligence of your mind is enormously diminished, although you might feel like you are seriously coming to grips with what's now in your life.

WHAT DO WE DO ABOUT IT?

Let's summarize. Life is lousy. We win some and we lose some. And we create the experience of unhappiness when we lose. If we uplevel our addictive demands to preferences, life can still be lousy—**but we don't make ourselves feel bad any longer.** The human mind is such an incredible instrument—a marvel of the universe—that it can become the master of its own experience.

This book will show you how to use the wonderful growth capacity of your mind. This capacity can enable your mind to change its programming instead of living out its present addictive demands for the rest of your life—like a robot. You can learn to enjoy your life no matter what's happening. It's simple—just uplevel addictions to preferences. However, doing it is not simple. It takes a basic knowledge of how the mind works, it takes a deep determination to do it, and it takes **continuous practice until new mental habits replace the old habits that have been developed over millions of years in our evolution from the jungle.** So how do you do it? It's only a first step to tell you that your life will be wonderful if you uplevel your addictive programming to preferential programming. To really do it, you need specific methods and tools that you can use to accomplish this inner work.

As you work on yourself, you can begin to experience that you can view yourself, the people with whom you interact and the whole world as a vast training laboratory that can help you become more conscious. Everyone and everything can become your teacher—whether they know it or not. All you need is your life! You'll discover that the life you are living is perfect in offering you teachings to give you the "grist for the mill" that you need in your long journey of upleveling addictions to preferences.

There are several techniques for doing this inner work. In this book, we will concentrate on explaining the use of The Twelve Pathways. As pointed out in my *Handbook to Higher Consciousness*, "The Twelve Pathways are a modern, practical condensation of thousands of years of accumulated wisdom. They give you a minute-to-minute guide for operating your consciousness while you interact with the world around you."*

The Twelve Pathways are systematically interwoven. Each implies the others. This increases their effectiveness

---

*The *Handbook to Higher Consciousness* presents an overview of the Living Love Way to increase your enjoyment and effectiveness in life. It can be ordered from Cornucopia Books, 790 Commercial Ave., Coos Bay, OR 97420 for $3.95 plus $1.25 for postage and handling. See Appendix 3.

in helping you get the most from your life. If you can perfectly live in the consciousness of any one Pathway, you will automatically be actualizing most of the others in your life!

So let's explore the Twelve Pathways together so that we can use them in our daily lives to help us to accomplish a seeming miracle—to increasingly enjoy ourselves no matter what is happening in our lives. When you read the next page, you may be taking the next step in what could be the greatest challenge and adventure of your life!

THE TWELVE PATHWAYS
To Unconditional Love and Happiness

FREEING MYSELF

1. I am freeing myself from security, sensation and power addictions that make me try to forcefully control situations in my life, and thus destroy my serenity and keep me from loving myself and others.

2. I am discovering how my consciousness-dominating addictions create my illusory version of the changing world of people and situations around me.

3. I welcome the opportunity (even if painful) that my minute-to-minute experience offers me to become aware of the addictions I must reprogram to be liberated from my robot-like emotional patterns.

BEING HERE NOW

4. I always remember that I have everything I need to enjoy my here and now—unless I am letting my consciousness be dominated by demands and expectations based on the dead past or the imagined future.

5. I take full responsibility here and now for everything I experience, for it is my own programming that creates my actions and also influences the reactions of people around me.

6. I accept myself completely here and now and consciously experience everything I feel, think, say and do (including my emotion-backed addictions) as a necessary part of my growth into higher consciousness.

INTERACTING WITH OTHERS

7. I open myself genuinely to all people by being willing to fully communicate my deepest feelings, since hiding in any degree keeps me stuck in my illusion of separateness from other people.

8. I feel with loving compassion the problems of others without getting caught up emotionally in their predicaments that are offering them messages they need for their growth.

9. I act freely when I am tuned-in, centered and loving, but if possible I avoid acting when I am emotionally upset and depriving myself of the wisdom that flows from love and expanded consciousness.

DISCOVERING MY CONSCIOUS-AWARENESS

10. I am continually calming the restless scanning of my rational mind in order to perceive the finer energies that enable me to unitively merge with everything around me.

11. I am constantly aware of which of the Seven Centers of Consciousness I am using, and I feel my energy, perceptiveness, love and inner peace growing as I open all of the Centers of Consciousness.*

12. I am perceiving everyone, including myself, as an awakening being who is here to claim his or her birthright to the higher consciousness planes of unconditional love and oneness.

*The Seven Centers of Consciousness are explained in Chapter 14.

PART II

Freeing Myself

I am freeing myself from security, sensation and power addictions that make me try to forcefully control situations in my life, and thus destroy my serenity and keep me from loving myself and others.

4

you are your own jailer

THE TWELVE PATHWAYS ARE not simple statements. They are directions for the operation of our complex human minds. These guidelines show us how to increase our energy, perceptiveness, wisdom, inner peace, love and happiness—which are sadly lacking in most of our lives.

The ideas in the Pathways are not new. They have roots in human experience that can be historically traced back thousands of years. They are in a form that talks to the rational mind. Yet if they're to help us get the most from our lives, we must learn to use them in a way that deeply resonates with the intuitive functioning of our minds. The Pathways are a handy package of **reminders of what you already know deep in your unconscious, intuitive wisdom.** When running an addictive program, your mind will override your intuitive wisdom that truly directs you toward love and enjoyment of life. But no matter how much you are resisting, clinging or ignoring, there is always a small inner voice that can be heard if you want to hear it. And these Twelve Pathways will constantly speak to this inner awareness, reinforcing it, and reminding your mind that its addictive programming cannot possibly bring you deep, lasting satisfaction.

INNER FREEDOM

Let's look at the first four words of the First Pathway: "I am freeing myself." They signal an enormous revolution within you. **They imply a determination to retrain your mind to no longer create the illusions of the separate-self.** These four words announce your intention to grow into **the higher consciousness of the unified-self.** (Remember the Glossary.) The words "I am freeing myself" recognize that you have been in a jail of your own creation—that your mind has been fettered by security, sensation and power addictions that greatly limit your ability to get the most from your life.

The beginning of the First Pathway also contains some good news. It indicates that **we can free ourselves.** Many of us have been hoping that our parents, our teachers, our lovers, our friends or the politicians would save us and help us live pleasant lives. The First Pathway begins on the high note that each person can do it for himself or herself.

Many of us are touchy about external constraints. We don't want anyone telling us what to do. The First Pathway suggests that **the most important freedoms are not external but internal freedoms.** In the melodrama of life, it

28

may be great to be married to someone who never tells us that we should take better care of the family car. But there will always be times in our lives when we are told what to do or not do. And that's why it is essential for our own happiness to uplevel our security, sensation and power addictions to preferences **so that we will not make ourselves feel separate or upset when a person tells us to take better care of the car.**

When our minds are programmed with addictions that activate the separate-self, we live in the illusion that external freedoms determine our happiness—and the vital matter of internal freedom is hardly recognized as important at all. Although we may want to play the game of resisting arbitrary and unneeded restrictions on how we play our roles in the melodrama of life, we begin to realize that **internal freedom is to be prized as vitally important in creating a satisfying life.**

It's simple. If you have external freedom but lack internal freedom, you will live an unhappy life. If you have internal freedom but lack external freedom, you can still live in an energetic, wise, perceptive, happy, loving and purposeful way.

THE MISERY WE CREATE

The First Pathway then reminds us what we are getting free from—"security, sensation and power addictions." As we discovered in the last chapter, these addictions make us automatically and compulsively resist, cling and ignore. They are destructive of the real capacity of our minds to integrate life energies so as to produce an effective and satisfying "flow" in our lives. Let's look closely at the many rip-offs that "the three poisons" bring into our lives when our separate-self is running addictive programming:

1. **Effects on the body.** On the body level, we experience tension, tightness, clumsiness, weakness, "accidents" and sometimes pain and illness. Preferential pro-

gramming permits us to see the overall unified picture and maintain a relaxed body.

2. **Walls of separateness.** Our security, sensation and power addictions trigger separating feelings of fear, frustration, anger, irritation, resentment, jealousy, boredom, etc. When we uplevel our addictions to preferences, our nervous systems no longer manufacture these separating emotions. We have an overview from a perspective that lets us create alternative experiences of love, joy, harmony and cooperativeness. This helps us respond more appropriately to anything we can change without creating more problems in our lives.

3. **Less love.** The resisting, clinging and ignoring caused by our emotion-backed demands make us unable to feel love for ourselves and other people. They may also blind us to the love coming our way, or they may keep us from accepting it.

4. **Judgmentalness.** Addictions spark the mind to become critical and judgmental, which gives us the limited "payoff" of "being right" but destroys our ability to be cooperative, harmonious and happy.

5. **Distorted perceptions.** When we are enmeshed in addictions, our perceptions are grossly distorted; we focus our attention on the "hole" and not on the "doughnut"; we fail to appreciate the beauty around us; and we create and live in a world of distortion and illusion with "unsolvable" problems. When we uplevel addictions to preferences, our minds can operate clearly; we can enjoy our here and now. We can respond more effectively to change what's changeable and let the rest go. We can enjoy the beauty and richness that is always available in every moment.

6. **Muffled creativity.** Security, sensation and power addictions destroy our spontaneity, creativity and

openness. Our minds become rigid rather than flexible. We will be limited in choices rather than creatively wide-ranging in finding effective solutions.

7. **Unhappiness.** When we are in the grip of addictively resisting, clinging and ignoring, we make ourselves unhappy. When our energy is wasted in this way, we will usually lack the enthusiasm, clear insight and wisdom to optimally flow our thoughts and actions into joyously playing the game of life. Instead, we experience life as a burdensome "problem" rather than an interesting "game" to play.

These seven rip-offs add up to a private hell that we create and inhabit. A mind caught up in security, sensation and power addictions will not experience serenity and happiness even when it gets what it thinks it must have. It will create only a temporary "egoey" pleasure. But the separate-self is insatiable. "What is" in life is never enough. There must be more. We compare our situations with others. And our minds usually escalate our demands if life begins to satisfy them. We are often unable to enjoy what we do have because **we become so preoccupied with protecting it—and increasing it.** We find it difficult to trust ourselves or the flow of energies in the environment around us. **We constantly run our addictive programming from minute to minute and thus CREATE A SOLID EXPERIENCE OF SEPARATENESS.** The effect of these addictions is an illusory duality of "me vs. the world" instead of the unified experience of "me and the world" and "me in the world."

ADDICTIONS ARE NOT SERIOUS

Although most of this book has mean things to say about addictions, it's good to remember that, behind it all, addictions aren't really serious! They have definite consequences in your life, but you don't have to be addicted to not having addictions. Of course, addictions create your separating experiences, but it's O.K. to be frustrated, angry, afraid or unhappy. It's just your mental habits—your programming. It's not really the essential you. It's all part of the role that you're playing at this point in your life. It's where you are right now in your journey of awakening. To be realistic, let's recognize that you probably won't uplevel all your addictive demands to preferences during your lifetime. What you can do is to learn to handle them more and more effectively so they don't churn up your life so much. You can increasingly learn to remember (you constantly forget!) that it's always your own addictions that create your experience—not "what is." You can take responsibility—but without blaming anyone—including yourself. And you can learn to observe the way your mind resists, clings and ignores. By using the Pathways, you can set the stage for your mind to increasingly accept, let go and remember. You can begin to script your life as a love drama—instead of a separating tragedy.

Although addictions aren't serious, addictive snarls are something else again. Single addictions can arise and pass away easily. For example you may addictively demand that someone not beat you into a parking space; later in the day the separating feelings will most likely be gone. However, multiple addictions often feed each other and crystallize into a spaghetti of intertwined addictive demands that mutually support a separating position.

Addictive snarls can fill your head with rocks of separateness. They deeply alter the flow of your life. They can progressively enlarge so as to taint more and more of your life. They are a part of your inner work that takes a high level of skill to successfully break up. Instead of having to deal with a light drizzle, they can create drenching storms for you to handle. Even so, always remember that behind all that, they are not serious—just part of your daily soap opera. Chapter 16 tells you how to work on your addictive snarls.

THREE CONSEQUENCES

The beginning of the First Pathway reminds us that we are in a jail of our own making, and signals our intention to work toward freedom ("I am freeing myself"). The second part of the Pathway specifies that we want freedom from our "security, sensation and power addictions." The remainder of the Pathway reminds us of three of the most potent reasons why we can no longer afford to let our lives be blighted by these addictions:

1. They "... make me try to forcefully control situations in my life ..."
2. "... and thus destroy my serenity ..."
3. "... and keep me from loving myself and others."

Let's look at the first point—forcefully controlling situations. When the mind is dominated by addictions, our freedom of choice is destroyed. The resources of the organism are compulsively funneled into a "survival" struggle to fulfill the addictive programming. This perceptual framework automatically plays out a "me-vs.-the world" melodrama. It creates a warlike frame of reference. Our illusion that life is a battle to get "enough" becomes a self-fulfilling prophecy of the separate-self.

The alternative to creating life as a battle is to direct the mind to create a panoramic insight into your addictive demands, and how they affect your ability to love yourself and others. The more addictions, the less emotional acceptance and love. As you become more accepting and loving of yourself and others, you will find that the energy of love produces a remarkable difference in your life. Instead of creating an experience of "me vs. the world" and "I have to fight for everything," the energy of love enables you to perceptually experience other people as "us" rather than "them." This in turn makes it easier for them to experience you as "us" in their perceptual field. This "us" consciousness helps you find that you get more than you need to en-

33

joy your life without having to struggle for it. And you let the rest go, since the nature of life is that you win some and you lose some.

Thus, you get enough—not by forcefully controlling situations in your life, but by loving yourself and others so unconditionally that an abundant life is created without struggle. When you try to forcefully control, you usually turn off the energy of people around you. When you love and serve the world, the energy of abundance automatically flows toward you.

DESTROYING SERENITY

The First Pathway offers you the insight that when you try to forcefully control situations in your life, you destroy your serenity. Let's look at why things work this way. Look back at situations in which your own anger often led people to create an experience of fear, or anger, or both. In one way or another, they resisted you in direct proportion to the amount of force you used. You found yourself caught up in an unexpected struggle of "you" vs. "him" or "her" or "them."

Since you felt you were right, you became righteously indignant—and applied even more force. Since their separate-selves were creating their own experience that **they** were right, they stepped up their resistance (psychologically and otherwise) and the serenity you had hoped to create by forcefully changing a situation was nowhere to be found. Instead the lack of perceptiveness, insight and wisdom created by your addictive programming interacting with the life situation resulted in turmoil both in your mind and the minds of other people.

When you uplevel addictions to preferences, it is possible to have a deep level of serenity inside—and yet be quite active on the outside. For example, if you're not addictively demanding that life be different from the way it is, you can be hurrying to get somewhere—and yet be feeling a relaxing inner peace. On the other hand, you can be sitting in a comfortable armchair and be disturbed, worried and anxious. Thus serenity is independent of the melodrama of life. It's a matter of keeping addictions down and love up.

When one goes down, the other goes up.

LOVING YOURSELF AND OTHERS

The last part of the First Pathway reminds you that security, sensation and power addictions "keep me from loving myself and others." You'll recall that addictions are defined as emotion-backed demands. Most people have hundreds of specific security, sensation and power addictions that they are living out in robot fashion. At a given moment in life, it is usual for our life conditions to be triggering one or more of these addictions. Because of this continuity of addictive activity, **we constantly create and solidify the illusion of the separate-self—me vs. the world.**

This intensive and continuous domination of your consciousness by your addictive demands **often keeps you from loving yourself.** This alienation from, and rejection of, yourself is one of the most penalizing ways to use your mind. **It represents the enormous power of the mind turned against itself.**

The programs of the mind that lead one to reject oneself can take such a beautiful guideline as "love everyone unconditionally" and use it as a way of lowering one's own self-esteem. "I'm terrible, I'm awful, I'm hopeless because I keep throwing people out of my heart." A mind that does not reject itself can hear the same guideline and say, "That sounds like the way I want to operate my life. Right now I'm angry at Mary, and I'm going to use this experience to work on myself. Experiencing my addictions helps me grow."

As long as your mind is using self-rejecting tapes, it can twist anything you do to reject you. It thereby protects itself from working on its addictive demands. It uses growth training as another way to self-reject. Because self-rejection slows you down in getting free of addictions in other areas (and also causes you much suffering in itself), it deserves a high priority in your inner work. Addictive demands you bear on yourself can be successfully worked on like all other addictions.

Almost everyone, in one degree or another, needs inner work in this area. You will tremendously enrich your experience of life by taking on self-acceptance as another part of your growth. **Challenge your mind to learn to be gentle with yourself and to emotionally accept and love yourself just the way you are—or just the way you aren't.**

TO SUM UP

Thus the First Pathway dynamically sets up the game of consciousness growth. It challenges one to work for freedom—and to view the most important freedom as **inner freedom.** It pinpoints the three main classes of addictions that keep our lives from being as satisfying as possible: security addictions, sensation addictions and power addictions. And then it reminds us of three ways in which our addictive programmings produce problems for us—forcefully controlling, destroying serenity and reducing love for oneself and others. Now it is the job of the remaining eleven Pathways to spell out the operational specifics whereby we can skillfully use our minds to get the most that is possible from our lives.

*I am discovering how my conscious-
ness-dominating addictions create my
illusory version of the changing world
of people and situations around me.*

5

breaking
through illusions

THE SECOND PATHWAY OPENS
with the fulfilling statement "I am discovering." The word
"discovering" implies that you are becoming aware of something that is already there. It is like discovering a treasure
that will add richness to your life.

The Second Pathway challenges us to discover in our
own lives the cause-effect relationship between our consciousness-dominating addictions and the illusory versions
that we create about ourselves and the world around us.
We know we have addictions, and we know we have illu-

sions or misunderstandings. **But we have not connected our addictions and our "mistakes" in a cause-effect relationship.** This lack of insight enables our ego-minds to blithely convince us that our illusions are due to a lack of "thinking," and that all we need to do to break through the illusions is to think more. The real culprit in the crime (our addictions) goes undetected.

DISTORTED PERCEPTION

How do we deepen our understanding of the way our perception is thrown off when we are running an addictive tape? We only need to contrast the dramatic difference in our experience of the world around us when (1) the mind is running an addictive demand and (2) the mind is running a preferential tape. Let's look at the diagram entitled "How Perception Is Distorted by Addictive Programming."

Perception is like a five-ring circus with lots of things happening at once. At any given moment, you can be aware of only a tiny portion of stuff going on in and around you. Selection is necessary. Whether you're using addictive or preferential programming determines **the type and amount of input** that will be projected onto the screen of your consciousness **and thus enter your awareness.**

You cannot be aware of everything simultaneously. You are only aware of that which is being selected here and now by your mind for projection onto the screen of your consciousness—that little TV screen somewhere inside your head on which you see images and also hear sounds, smell smells, taste tastes, feel feelings and notice thoughts and emotions.

Now let's examine the five components of our perceptive mix:

1. **"What Is."** Of the five types of input material, one of them, "What Is," deals with that which is both outside and inside of our skin here and now. The other four (emotional feelings, memories of the past, future

HOW PERCEPTION IS DISTORTED BY ADDICTIVE PROGRAMMING

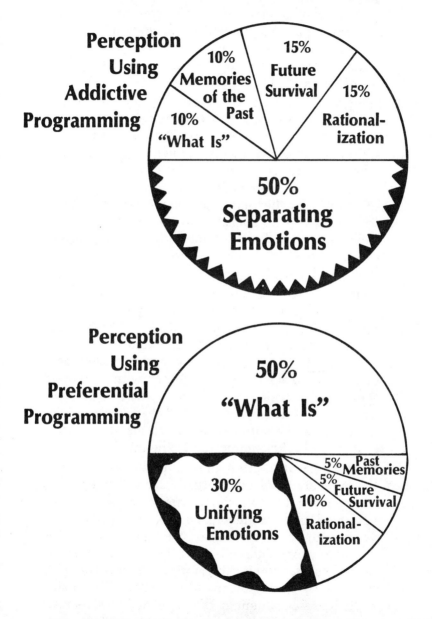

Perception Using Addictive Programming

10% Memories of the Past

15% Future Survival

15% Rationalization

10% "What Is"

50% Separating Emotions

Perception Using Preferential Programming

50% "What Is"

5% Past Memories

5% Future Survival

10% Rationalization

30% Unifying Emotions

The diagrams above represent a generalization of how motivational intensity affects your perception. The percentages will vary depending on the strength of the addictive or preferential programming and the life situation.

survival and rationalization) all refer to what you are creating at this moment inside your skin. "What Is" is all that is solid here and now—all of the other factors in the diagram are thoughts and feelings that are produced by the mind.

2. **Emotions.** You'll notice in the diagram that when the mind is unbalanced by addictive programming, 50 percent of your awareness may be claimed by your separating emotions of fear, anger, frustration, etc. When you are using preferential programming and are not creating separating emotions inside you, the space taken by these emotions on your screen of consciousness can be available for unifying emotional feelings, such as love, serenity, joy and happiness— and can also help your perception of "what is" to be increased from 10% to 50%!

3. **Memories of the Past.** Another input source that your mind must deal with in determining your perceptive mix at each moment is labeled "Memories of the Past" in the diagram. Each of us has extensive memory banks in which we have filed away an incredible mass of material from the past together with associated thoughts and feelings. These obviously interact with the rationalizing functions to add even more individual flavor and emotional variety to the mental stew that is constantly simmering in the mind.

4. **Future Survival.** Although rationalizing functions of the mind are involved, "Future Survival" deserves its own place in the five-ring circus of perception. The ego-mind understandably puts a high priority on your future survival. Whatever tape your mind is running, your mind will instantly push the override button so that you quickly notice anything that may have a bearing on your future survival. When using addictive programming, the mind will erroneously treat as a survival matter many things that have

Second Pathway: I am discovering how my consciousness-dominating addictions create
my illusory version of the changing world of people
and situations around me.

nothing to do with your survival. This often keeps
you worried over things that really aren't important
when seen with insight and perspective.

5. **Rationalization.** Another part of the five-ring circus
(from which your mind must select that which comes
into your awareness) is referred to in the diagram as
"Rationalization." This refers to the capacity of your
intellect—or rational mind—to produce an infinity of
thoughts to back up your addictions and preferences.
In playing its game, the rational mind uses numerous
categories, such as good or bad, true or false, beautiful
or ugly, efficient or inefficient, fast or slow, and of
course, its favorite polarity of **right or wrong.**

A part of the activity of the mind is to fit what's
now into various classifications. "The movie is boring."
"The sunset is beautiful." It can go on forever, churning out separating distinctions, barbed comparisons,
right-wrong judgments and cutting criticisms, as well
as approvals and pats on the back. And you sometimes
need the intellect to run off its discriminations. For
example, it may need to tell you whether someone can
or can't handle a job. Somehow you've got to be able to
use your rational mind—and at the same time not
throw yourself out of the love space.

Just as dogs need to be housebroken, your mind must be
trained to do its work without messing up your life. And
your intellect can be trained to operate without interfering
with the heart space you want to create with yourself—
and other people. Regardless of whether it gets you into
positions that are right or wrong, if you have skillfully
trained your mind, it can do its thing and yet avoid trap-
ping you in emotional separateness.

How do you train your mind? You do it by using the Pathways to uplevel addictions to preferences. A daily practice
that will help you operate your mind more skillfully is explained in Chapter 16.

ADDICTIONS THROW OFF THE BALANCE

When the mind begins to run an addictive tape, the balance of certain input factors of perception is enormously altered. Notice in the diagram how separating emotional feelings dominate half of the perceptive input. When we run an addiction, our bodies can create headache, tension in the neck, tightness in the chest, lower back pain, upset stomach, high blood pressure, ulcers, etc. Enjoyable feelings or neutral feelings are replaced by anger, fear, jealousy, resentment, irritation, worry, grief, frustration, disdain, boredom and many, many other separating emotions that when prolonged, create the experience we recognize as unhappiness.

These separating emotional feelings spark the rational mind to justify, rationalize and keep us trapped in our addictive demands. We lose balance, perspective and wisdom when our rational minds are focused on making ourselves right and others wrong. We will burst into a diarrhea of words as the ego defends the real or implied threat to our addictive territories. Thus the diagram shows an enlargement of the activity of the rational mind when it is being driven by an addiction.

The rational mind is not a truth-seeking instrument. Truth is a function of your intuitive wisdom already within you. When running addictions, the doors of your perception will be closed to subtle clues that the communications you are making do not accurately point to "what is." In most cases when you're running an addiction, your rational mind is mainly concerned with making itself right and others wrong.

Perhaps the greatest distortion comes from the enormous reduction in the "what is" area of perception. This is especially distorting because the mind has the illusion that it is accurately tuned-in to "what is." When operating an addiction, the mind will tend to perceive only that which affects the current addictive demand it is running. Thus, instead of having a three-hundred-and-sixty-degree mountaintop view of "what is," the perceptive mechanisms of our minds create a "tunnel vision." Let's review how the addictive mode of perception continually harms us. As addictive programming is activated, the mind is cutting down its alertness to "what is" in our lives and is turning up its emotional "whips" to drive us into "fight or flight." Separating emotional feelings are emphasized in our perceptive field, and our overall view of the world is diminished. The mind no longer wisely and intuitively integrates "what's now" in our lives. Instead, it is dominated by the overload caused by the powerful energy streams of such emotions as anger, fear and jealousy.

When the world is not conforming with the addictive demands programmed into our minds, our mental machinery acts like a 110-volt vacuum cleaner that mistakenly got plugged into a 220-volt outlet. The result is neurosis—which is normal in our culture.

Preferential programming enables our minds to function in an insightful way that helps us harmonize relevant factors and get the most that's gettable in our lives. **When we run addictive programs, molehills become mountains, and mountains are often ignored.** There is no end to the illusions that an addiction can produce.

And there is no limit to how we can make self-fulfilling prophecies out of these illusions. If we have the illusion that someone hates us, we will then most likely feel, think, say and do things that indicate how separate we feel from this person. It should then come as no great surprise to find that this person will accurately fulfill our prophecy that s/he hates us. Thus the mind can make itself "right" even when it's "wrong."

THE CHANGING WORLD

The Second Pathway also reminds us that one of the basic characteristics of the world we live in, and of the

43

bodies and minds we inhabit, is that everything is a changing process. The rate of change may be fast or slow. Everything is composed of atoms—or energy, such as light or heat. On the atomic level, what exists is the dynamic dance of atoms and electrons in such a rapid rate of change that any image of how things are becomes obsolete within a split second.

Although our bodies are changing every moment with new cells being born and other cells dying, we usually don't notice much difference in their appearance or performance if we compare today with yesterday. But comparisons over the years or decades can make us aware that our bodies are also changing processes. The Statue of Liberty in New York Harbor changes more slowly than, for example, our human bodies. But even this metal statue is gradually corroding, so that its life is limited—although it may last longer than you or me.

RAPIDLY AGING FACTS

The Second Pathway ends with a reminder that it is people that change and situations that change—just about everything in your life! Your mind often latches onto "rapidly aging" facts with such an addictive grip that you ignore the process-nature of the world.

When you are running an addiction, the tones of your voice and the vibrational space you project may imply that you know all there is to know about a given subject. But even if your information is adequate, how can you ever be sure that things have not changed (or cannot change in the future) in a way that will make your dogmatic utterances quite inappropriate? Emerson said, "In nature every moment is new; the past is always swallowed and forgotten; the coming only is sacred . . . . People wish to be settled; only as far as they are unsettled is there any hope for them." Scientist and philosopher Alfred North Whitehead viewed the problem succinctly, "Knowledge keeps no better than fish."

Our minds can erect a pride and prestige boundary around us that destroys our receptivity and our ability to update our information. We are unable to hear the messages life is giving us. This inflexibility will not happen if we can avoid becoming addictively identified with the information in our memory banks. Instead we can stay open-minded and remain fully attuned to the changing world of people and situations around us. In this way, our minds can help us enjoy our full potential.*

Thus the Second Pathway helps us remember that as our addictions go up, our insight, understanding, and even factual accuracy head downward. Distorted facts and separating judgmentalness churn away inside the mind and feed upon each other. Our minds become fascinated with crystallizing and building a case that confirms the separate-self. And the price we pay in lost happiness is too much. We can use the Second Pathway to patiently remind us of the illusions that are being spun out by our addictive programming. And these insights help us take one more step toward enjoying our lives—in spite of it all.

*You may wish to read my book *Taming Your Mind*. It discusses techniques that can improve the operation of the rational mind to increase its awareness of "what is." It contains "tools for thinking" that help the mind self-correct its tendency to create errors and illusions. It may be ordered from Cornucopia Books, 790 Commercial Ave., Coos Bay, OR 97420 for $7.95 (clothbound) plus $1.25 for postage and handling.

I welcome the opportunity (even if painful) that my minute-to-minute experience offers me to become aware of the addictions I must reprogram to be liberated from my robot-like emotional patterns.

6

your life is your teacher

IT IS A LONG EVOLUTIONARY journey from the animal state to the human state. The mutations that created our species (*homo sapiens*) increased the number of cortical cells in our brains—thereby adding language and conceptual capacity. Anthropological records indicate that *homo sapiens* evolved about 50,000 years ago. If we figure approximately four generations per century, this means that you and I are about the two thousandth generation of our species. We're all pioneers in the evolutionary journey of humankind!

Just as it is a long journey from the animal to the human state, it is an intricate journey from where we are now to what we will call "the awakened" state. An awakened person goes through life choosing actions that add to love and unity when past, present and probable future consequences are increasingly seen with the panoramic insight of the unified-self—rather than the self-conscious tunnel vision of the separate-self. And the good news is that you and I can progress toward this in our lifetime if we understand what it is we are doing.

THE SPLIT BETWEEN SELF AND OTHER

What we're doing is **learning to operate this remarkable mind that permitted our emergence from the animal state.** The mind of an animal will constantly trigger fear when it experiences anything that might be threatening, will compulsively push toward satisfying desires for food and sex and will automatically create hostility when its territory is invaded. Jungle situations constantly trigger security, sensation and power consciousness in animals—and these responses are appropriate to life in the wild.

Similarly most humans are creating a hurricane of "me vs. the world," and are constantly triggering fear, frustration and anger. This split, created by the separate-self programming inherited from the jungle, constantly rips off our bodies with psychosomatic tension, worry and anxiety. An animal whose territory is invaded will respond by rapidly increased heartbeat, adrenalin going into the bloodstream and glycogen mobilized from the liver to give quick energy to the muscles. The entire nervous system will be prepared for flight or fight. And in running or fighting, the animal discharges the energies that readied it for the survival emergency.

In our civilized melodrama, we don't often have an actual threat to our lives, but our nervous systems continually trigger the experience of threat—even if a person only throws a critical word toward us. And then we simmer in our emotional juices instead of healthily working them off in physical activity like the animals. Instead of being open, alert, awake and here-and-now, we become neurotic, anxious, serious and dominated by worrying thoughts. Life ceases to be a delightful game to play with an experience of awe, wonder, beauty and the fun and mystery of what will happen next. Instead it becomes a heavy, problem-filled struggle to get enough security, sensation and power.

Fight or flight is the natural, compulsive response of an animal and "unawake human beings" in situations that trigger addictions. Our mental habits make us assume that our experience is caused by what others are doing or saying. Our moment-to-moment experience of life is not usually seen as being **primarily, immediately and practically** caused by our own programming and ways of habitually responding—and secondarily caused by "what is." Instead, the mind locks onto the outside event which we try to forcefully change or run away from. As long as we respond to painful life situations that trigger our emotions of anger, fear, jealousy, resentment, irritation and boredom **by only trying to change "what is" in our lives,** we are greatly limiting ourselves.

We need a two-handed approach to getting the most from our lives. On one hand we can try to change the outside world. And on the other hand, **we need to be able to skillfully change our internal responses to "what is" in our lives.**

USING PAIN FOR GROWTH

The Third Pathway advises us to "welcome the opportunity (even if painful) that my minute-to-minute experience offers me to become aware of the addictions ...." The experience of fear, frustration or anger **now becomes a helpful guide** to spotting and eliminating the cancerous programmings in our minds that make us create a world of separateness instead of a world of unity.

Third Pathway: I welcome the opportunity (even if painful) that my minute-to-minute experience offers me to become aware of the addictions I must reprogram to be liberated from my robot-like emotional patterns.

When we live in the consciousness of the Third Pathway, the emotionally painful parts of life **are seen as opportunities** to "become aware of the addictions I must reprogram to be liberated from my robot-like emotional patterns." What we've previously treated as horrible and terrible, **we now "magically" transform into a stepping stone for our growth.** Life becomes our helpful friend! All ways! Always!

We're not masochists—we don't welcome psychological pain for the sake of pain. When it happens, instead of resisting, we welcome pain or unhappiness as cogent pointers to that which we are addictively resisting in our lives which will continue to create pain until we reprogram the separate-self addictive demands that make us vulnerable when this life condition happens.

The Third Pathway helps you experience this new way of seeing the usefulness of pain and unhappiness **if you will only use them for your growth.** It reminds you that a mind that is running addictive tapes is like a robot. It lacks choice and flexibility. It mechanically and automatically responds with anger or fear. Look at the last time you created the experience of anger or fear in your life. You did not decide to become angry or afraid—**it automatically happened when your addictive programming neurologically stimulated the limbic area in your brain** to produce patterns of emotional response in your body and mind.

TEACHERS AND LOVERS

If you are to "welcome the opportunity" and use all of the situations in your life as stepping stones on your journey of awakening, you will need a new attitude toward people and situations in your life. Instead of perceiving them in a subject-object manner and compulsively trying to change them, you begin to experience them as "teachers." We use the term "teacher" to refer to someone or something that puts you in touch with one of your addictive programmings. This is usually unintentional. But whether intentional or not, you can use the situation to formulate what you are addictively demanding and get to work on upleveling it to a preference.

Suppose someone says something you don't like, and you create the automatic addictive response of anger. Instead of lashing out angrily and making him/her wrong, you just note that s/he is offering you a "teaching." S/he is only sending energy your way that helps you get in touch with your addictive programming that creates your vulnerability—and keeps you trapped in these vestiges of the animal state. Then you use your energy in an on-the-spot mental practice described in Part VI. When emotions are running high, instead of tearing into other people, you can use this energy to work on your addictions. You can learn to greatly accelerate your growth through this insight method energized by your emotions.

The Living Love Methods of consciousness growth will help you experience everybody in your life as either a teacher or a lover. When people say or do things that make you trigger fear, frustration, anger or any feelings of separateness, they are acting as your teacher whether they know it or not. They are giving you the opportunity to use the Pathways to deal with your addictions that distort your experience of yourself and the world. And when they are not triggering your addictions, you get to experience them as "lovers."

In this context, the word "lover" does not refer to a sexual partner. I would like to see this friendly term come into general use to indicate anyone to whom your heart is open. A person is a lover to the degree that you have eliminated within your mind the walls of separateness between you and that person.

One way to look at the consciousness growth game is that it involves changing "teachers" into "lovers." And this is done by working on yourself. In the past we've done our best to modify people by trying to change what they say and do so that it fits our addictive programmings—so we could love them. And in spite of our best efforts for most of our lives, the people around us have not changed that much! Now we're going to try a new strategy that will really work. In addition to working on people around us, we're going to work on ourselves. We're going to use our minds to handle our own addictions—and to work toward upleveling our addictive demands into preferences **so that we can create the experience of love no matter what people say or do.** Although this is really hard work, it is not as tough as trying to change what people say and do—or living with our volatile addictions for the rest of our lives. And the nice thing about working on our addictions is that it is totally within our control and ability. The only cooperation we need is our own!

It will work best if you don't get caught up in spiritual pride and boast about how conscious you are becoming. You will find that people will notice a change in you without your advertising it. Just quietly welcome every opportunity that life offers you to spot the addictions that you have yet to uplevel to preferences. Don't miss any opportunity to practice taking your finger off the addiction button and putting it on the love button.

When we begin to view separating feelings as offering us a "teaching," we discover that everyone and everything can help us on our way in doing the inner work. Fathers, mothers, children, bosses, workers, friends, wives and husbands generally offer us most of our better"teachings." Our automobiles, our stereo sets, the leaking roofs on our houses, our job situations and even the aches and pains in our bodies can all offer us "teachings" to uplevel our addictions into preferences.

As we more deeply internalize the Third Pathway, we transform our "enemies" into "helpers" needed for our consciousness growth—and they don't even have to know what's happening! In fact, we will grow faster if they continue to do the same things that in the past have put us in touch with our addictive anger or fear! They actually help us get free when they continue doing whatever it is they're doing **so that we can use the experience to become aware of the addictions we must reprogram to be liberated from our robot-like emotional patterns.** Our experience of life will become light and satisfying when we deeply welcome the opportunity that **everything in our lives offers us either to work on ourselves to uplevel addictions to preferences or to experience the enjoyment of living.** We begin to see the **incredible perfection of everyone and everything around us**—and how all that happens helps us on our way.

The Third Pathway ends by reminding us that our addictions are keeping us trapped in "robot-like emotional patterns." We have not been exercising our human capacity to become **a creative cause** of our experience. Instead, our jungle-like programming makes us **an effect of "what is."** By verifying this as we watch our minds work in daily life situations, we open the door to go beyond this unskillful and unsatisfying way of operating our minds.

AN EXCITING CHALLENGE

The consciousness growth game is the most exciting challenge you could ever take on. Most life games are like child's play in comparison with the task of successfully handling one's addictions—and perhaps upleveling many of them to preferences. The inner work that is required on your mind is somewhat akin to pulling yourself up by your bootstraps—except that although it is difficult, it can be done. And the satisfying results are worth all of the energy that you put into your growth. Working on yourself is a lot easier than living out a whole lifetime of your addictive programming. Nothing is more tragic than a human life that is continually stuck in the addictive mode of fearfully and angrily demanding to change "what is" without the option of skillfully handling its addictive programming—and then **lovingly** putting energy into changing "what is."

The people who can rapidly and deeply use the attitude expressed in the Third Pathway are lucky indeed! **For even though we may not have upleveled a single addiction to a preference yet, just welcoming situations for growth can lighten by about half the weight of fear, frustration and anger that we ordinarily create.** When we "welcome the opportunity (even if painful)," our egos and minds do not make us feel quite as separate and unloving as we felt before. When we genuinely "welcome the opportunity" and we clearly see that it is our addictive programming that is making us feel separate, the flow of our energy begins to change. We tend to work on ourselves rather than automatically acting out hostility, hurt or avoidance. Our relationships begin to improve. We may still be triggering feelings of fear and anger, but we know that **it is our own addictive programming that is doing it to us.**

It is a part of the perfection of life that in this beginning part of our growth we can rapidly lighten some of the heaviness we've been creating in our lives. We don't have to wait for years to get some benefits that reinforce us and help us experience that what we're doing will enrich our lives.

SOCIAL IMPROVEMENT

An illusory view of consciousness growth is that it is somehow a withdrawal of energy from doing one's part toward working for social betterment. If you love everyone and work on your addictions that make you angry toward people, why would you ever want to do anything about anything?

Perhaps we should first see that **everybody's addictions are the real problem!** It's not you or me or our brothers and sisters on this planet. It is always security, sensation or power addictions that lead people to feel unaccepting, uncaring and unloving toward the creatures on this earth, the environment or each other. A very direct, practical way to improve our social environment is for you and me to work on our own heads to uplevel our own addictions to preferences. People will notice how we handle our addictive demands— especially if we're getting results. They will become aware that it is possible to increase our love and to wisely deal with our addictions without blaming others for our experience. They may wish to try out our "tools" for handling our addictive demands. Loving energy and good vibes are contagious!

In the long run, doing our inner work may have the greatest planetary consequences in helping all of us complete our escape from jungle consciousness. And what better way is there to work on ourselves than to flow our energy into social service, and at the same time, use these confronting situations to do our inner work? Let's write letters, carry placards and attend meetings to further social action, **and let's simultaneously use these situations to work on ourselves using the Twelve Pathways.**

As we work on ourselves, we can increasingly see with perspective all the stuff that four billion of us are creating as part of our long journey from the security, sensation and power consciousness of the jungle. Remember, we're all pioneers in the great adventure of civilizing ourselves. The first cities were built about eight thousand years ago—only about three hundred generations ago. From this vantage point, we can compassionately honor it all. And at the same time, we can flow our energy into social action. Thus social action and our inner work actually complement each other— and help each other become more effective.*

From a mountaintop perspective, we can see with love and compassion the difficulties and suffering in the current stage of our social evolution. Then from an "us" space, we

*Appendix 4 entitled "A Career in Loving and Serving the World" tells how you can get in touch with the staff program which I have established. In this program, you can help to build a better world by teaching the Living Love Way explained in this book.

can use our lives to love and serve the world by saying to ourselves and fellow human beings, "If we all cooperate together, this is the type of world we can create." And if our energy is reinforced by the energy of other people, we've got a "let's improve the world" game working. If we operate under the illusion that social action requires us to **throw people out of our hearts,** we are simply adding to the separateness and alienation in a world that we are doing our best to improve. For every step forward, we take half a step backward.

ANGER AND HATRED ARE UNSKILLFUL

We can notice ways in which we—and the world around us—still have unfinished business. We can play the game of improving ourselves and the world without losing the balanced picture of our lives and our civilization as evolving processes. A doctor does not have to hate the human body, or make himself mad over its imperfections, in order to remove a diseased appendix. If a doctor chooses, s/he can experience the beauty, the wonder and the marvelous aspects of our physical bodies and at the same time act to correct a condition that is causing illness. We can learn to be gentle, understanding and compassionate with ourselves—and our brothers and sisters on this planet.

Social reform does not have to be fueled by righteous anger and hatred. The most skillful social service flows from the motivation of loving and serving the world. Your service will have the highest level of long-term effectiveness when your experience of loving everyone remains steady and unflickering **even (or especially) while you are trying to shape up their act.**

Remember, you don't necessarily like their "act." **You love the actors. After all, it's all us—us brothers and sisters just playing out our programmed roles.** When your attempt to help the world is mixed in with addictive energies of fear, anger or hate, you may make some improvements—but you will miss out on the real game.

Addictions are always the root cause of war, environmental rip-off, economic exploitation and prejudice. As the late Harvard sociologist Dr. Pitirim Sorokin observed, the only way we can really get at the basic cause of our social problems is for us to liberate ourselves from the programming of the separate, selfish self—and to learn to cooperate in a loving, unified way to build better individual lives and better forms of living together on our planet.

Addictions are contagious and they lead us to treat our brothers and sisters on this planet in uncaring, unloving, cruel and selfish ways. As we free our energy from a preoccupation with our addictive separate-selves, we transform our experience of other people. As our unified-selves begin to flower, we can open ourselves to viewing people as "us" instead of "them." We can skillfully help them get their lives to work better. As Werner Erhard has expressed it so clearly:

> We can choose to make the success of all humanity our personal business. We can choose to be audacious enough to take responsibility for the entire human family. We can choose to make our love for the world what our lives are really about.
>
> Each of us now has the opportunity, the privilege, to make a difference in creating a world that works for all of us. It will require courage, audacity and heart. It is much more radical than a revolution—it is the beginning of a transformation in the quality of life on our planet. You have the power to fire "the shot heard 'round the world."
>
> If not you, who?
> If not now, when?
> If not here, where?

PART III

Being Here Now

I always remember that I have everything I need to enjoy my here and
now—unless I am letting my consciousness be dominated by demands
and expectations based on the dead
past or the imagined future.

7

you're rich but don't know it

MOST OF THE THOUGHTS
that are produced by our minds and most of the actions
that inevitably follow from these thoughts are motivated
by the desire to increase our happiness. The mind stays in
the grip of so many addictive demands that it constantly
puts off living in the now. It keeps busy "pasting" and
"futuring." And yet happiness can only happen in the
eternal now moment! There is no way you can be happy
"tomorrow"—for "tomorrow" literally will never arrive.
What we mean by "tomorrow" can only be experienced

when it becomes "now." **Life is a succession of now moments.**

The problem, of course, is not that there is something wrong with our minds. The key to the situation lies in the addictive programming that the mind is being required to cope with. It is this programming that is constantly side-tracking our enjoyment of the here and now while we deal with supposed "threats." In this way the mind misses out on experiencing the beauty that is available in every now moment.

With addictive programming, the mind usually stays busy ringing the emergency "alarm bell"—and we have to live with it. **We constantly create the illusion that when we get these emotion-backed demands met, then, at last, we can be happy!** But happiness never really happens for any deeply satisfying period of time—**our minds have so many addictions that this process just keeps repeating itself.** Consciously noticing and enjoying what is now in our lives is only an occasional happening rather than a usual experience.

The Fourth Pathway (like all the other Pathways) tries to help us break through the mental tyranny that is created by our addictive programmings. We are thus reminded, "I always remember that I have everything I need to enjoy my here and now . . . ." Our illusion that we can be happy when certain addictive demands are satisfied is so solid that our minds steadily sacrifice the possibility of happiness now. It's like the donkey with a carrot dangling before him—always pursuing but seldom attaining. "I've got problems." "If only . . . ." "There are things I need to do to feel good." "I'll be so happy when . . . ."

Yes. Yes. Yes. All of these things are a part of your experience that you are creating. But do you realize that **there has hardly ever been a time in your life when you weren't saying, "I could be happy if only . . . ."**? Can you see that during most of the hours of the remaining years of

Fourth Pathway: I always remember that I have everything I need to enjoy my here and now—
unless I am letting my consciousness be dominated by demands and
expectations based on the dead past or the imagined future.

your life, your mind can keep on creating a problem-filled experience? And do you realize that it's only the way in which you operate your mind that keeps you trapped in this *cul-de-sac*—the dead end that your addictive programming continually creates?

If you begin the long process of rooting out addictive programmings and replacing them with preferences, you'll still have lots of things to attend to in your life. But you won't experience them as "problems"—**they'll be experienced as part of the challenge—and opportunity—of life.** When you play a game of checkers, do you experience it as a heavy, threatening problem—or do you experience it as a fun game to play with lots of challenges?

Ah . . . You think checkers isn't serious—and life is? Wouldn't you like to be able to operate your mind so that you can play all of your life as a game—and live even more effectively? You would no longer burden your nervous system with all of the fear, anxiety, worry, anger, jealousy, resentment and boredom that you have been creating by the usual operation of your mind.

YOUR MIND IS "PERFECT"

Always remember that your mind is "perfect"—it is only the addictive programming that is creating the problem. It is vital that you separate the "machinery" of your mind (which is excellent) from the particular programs that it plays out (which are causing problems).

Imagine a million-dollar computer—a wonderful instrument. Likewise, your mind is a wonderful instrument—worth more than a million dollars! But a computer by itself will not operate. It needs programmed instructions—or, as we put it, games to play. Now let's suppose that the instructions that you put into this marvelous computer are self-contradictory and unskillful. If you put garbage in, you'll get garbage out! The wondrous functioning of your fine biocomputer can be nullified into garbage production if it is not appropriately programmed.

When we run off addictive programs, we constantly create confusion. We are beautiful and lovable—but the feelings, thoughts, words and actions produced by our minds when running off addictions create hell in our lives. But even this experience of "hell" may be regarded as O.K.— for it screamingly points to the ways in which we need to update our programming. We can use it for our growth.

The mind is like a fine stereo set on which we put a scratchy, bad-sounding record (our addictive programming). Since the stereo set is excellent, **it will excellently reproduce the lousy record.** Since our minds are excellent, they excellently reproduce the separating, addictive programming that we have picked up and are carrying around in our journey through life. Consciousness growth will occur most rapidly when we open ourselves to seeing how beautiful we really are—when we understand our basic inner goodness. To increase our level of enjoyment, all we need is to **learn to recognize and handle our addictive demands.** Then as our next step, we can work toward up-leveling our addictive programming into preferential programming to further increase our happiness level.

PASTING AND FUTURING

When we turn up our perception of what's now in our lives, we always have enough to enjoy our here and now. The problem is that **we are not usually tuning-in to what's really now in our lives.** Our minds become so dominated by our addictive demands that **we literally block out or ignore all of the beautiful aspects of the reality around us.** We look at the sourness of the lemon and forget that, with a little doing, we can make lemonade. We look at the hole— and fail to fully appreciate the doughnut.

It's as though we were visiting the magic environment of Disneyland, but our attention is mainly on a bunion on our big toe. Or we've chosen to go to a fine French restaurant, but all during the exotic meal our consciousness is dominated by what it is costing. Or we could be with our lover and sexual energy is running high, but we keep rehashing the argument we had at dinner tonight.

The Fourth Pathway reminds us, ". . . I have everything I need to enjoy my here and now—unless I am letting my consciousness be dominated by demands and expectations based on the dead past or the imagined future." When we are running addictive tapes about the dead past, we let our minds make us unhappy by contrasting how nice something was in the past compared with right now. This, of course, is an illusion because if we look at the whole of our experience in the past, our addictions were then keeping our minds worried and preoccupied. Let's look at some of the ways our minds may addictively trap us in "pasting" and "futuring."

If our minds have self-rejecting tapes, they may remain dominated by brooding about how "I didn't take advantage of the opportunities of the past." "If I had only known yesterday what I know today . . . ." When we addictively blame or reject ourselves, "Monday morning quarterbacking" represents a sickness of the mind. But sorting out the lessons our lives offer us can be a positive activity of the mind when we use our experiences to improve our life skills. Instead of rejecting ourselves, we can make ourselves feel richer because of the "mistakes" we have made and the experiences we have gained.

Our addictive tapes can make our minds create unpleasant experiences by comparing the good in the past with what's now in our lives. Or they may project thought forms of how much better our future can be than the present moment is. This is a very seductive tape for the mind to run. The rational mind constantly keeps itself in business by enticing us, "Rely on me, baby, and I'll get you there." It seldom reminds us that we have been relying on it—and look what it has done to us! It keeps on running tape after tape that makes us create the experience of being unhappy with ourselves, the people around us and the life conditions around us.

And there is no limit to how much criticalness, judgmentalness and dissatisfaction our minds can create about ourselves and the world we live in. Every book we read can make us more discriminating and give the mind more ways of separating "this" from "that." Whenever we tune-in to "the news," we are usually barraged with information designed to stimulate the critical tapes in our minds. We can select from the life facts around us so as to produce the experience that we're living in a "horror story." Or we can see things from a panoramic perspective and appreciate all of the beautiful things that we have created both in ourselves and in our environment—and still honor the messages life is giving us to "shape up our act."

USING THE FOURTH PATHWAY

Let's see how we can apply the Fourth Pathway to a life situation. Suppose your mind has security programming that makes it addictively cling to the job you now have. Here's a script of the soap opera you may create if you are fired from your job. Your addictive demands in this area of your life can make you trigger instant fear—followed by anger. You may make the boss wrong, may call him ugly names in your inner consciousness (if not verbally aloud) and may regard this as a terrible crisis in your life. You have mortgage payments and a family to support, and your mind may make you create the experience that this could be the tragic blow that does you in.

Your addictive programming will want to make you right and the company wrong. You'll want to tell all your friends

Fourth Pathway: I always remember that I have everything I need to enjoy my here and now—
unless I am letting my consciousness be dominated by demands and
expectations based on the dead past or the imagined future.

how horrendously the company treated you, and you'll
want to do everything you can to create ill will toward your
employer. While in the grip of the addictive demand that
you not lose your job, your mind may give you many sleep-
less nights. Most likely the tension and emotional upset
will soon result in weakened resistance in your body, and
you will make yourself sick.

When you go for interviews for a new job, your mind
may be so resentful and angry that it will focus on telling
the interviewer how badly you were treated by your previous company. Your mind will probably insist on making
you right and your former employer wrong. The interviewer is really not interested in your addictive anger with
the other company—instead he wants to get the feeling of
what you could contribute to his firm. The psychic space
that you are creating by running off your addictive programming will tend to make you unattractive to job inter-
viewers. And your difficulty in getting a new job may
trigger even more addictions that deepen your fear and
anger. You won't be able to see the opportunity that life is
giving you to perhaps get an even better job—or a job that
you enjoy more even if the pay is a little less.

CREATING THE EXPERIENCE OF ENOUGHNESS

If you had been able to use the Fourth Pathway consistently during this entire episode in your life, you could have
created a very different experience. Let's suppose that
within two seconds after you were notified that you were
fired, your mind had run the tape "I always remember that
I have everything I need to enjoy my here and now—unless
I am letting my consciousness be dominated by demands
and expectations based on the dead past or the imagined
future." If your mind were trained to use this Fourth Pathway tape, you could have gone home, shared the news with
your family and then gone out to dinner to celebrate!

And what do you have to celebrate when you've been fired? You have your life. You have you! And you have a loving world around you that will flow love your way.

In the enjoyment of celebrating your life that evening, you can look at your situation with your family. You've checked on the amount of unemployment income you have. You compare this with your money obligations. With your family, you make a decision regarding whether you or your mate should seek a temporary job to fill in. Perhaps if you have some vacation money saved, this may be a fine time to take several weeks off. Or maybe you'll use this opportunity to get things done around the house that you've been wanting to do for a long time.

In the meantime, you make a list of other companies with whom you wish to apply for a new job. You talk with your friends to find out as much as you can about these companies. You don't get sick—because you're really enjoying what's happening—and you appreciate the mini-vacation life is offering you. You're getting a chance to do a lot of things that you were usually too busy to do.

You know that you are a worthwhile person with useful job and personality skills. Somewhere there's a job waiting for you—and you get to play the game of finding it. You do not experience any threat because you know that you **are** enough, and that you always **have** enough to enjoy your here and now. By using the Fourth Pathway, your mind avoids creating the experience of a big crisis in your life. Instead you just see your life unfolding in an unexpected but, no doubt, beautiful way. You find no need to direct negativity and separateness toward your previous employer, yourself or the world. It's all a melodrama that we actors and actresses are playing with each other.

Because of your positive vibrations, you will most likely get a job before too long. And using the Third Pathway, you will see the entire soap opera as a way to check out your addictions—and work on them if you need to. Using the Fourth Pathway, you do not get stuck in the illusion that life is treating you terribly. You again experience that you have enough to enjoy your here and now. The Fourth Pathway affirms that your life can be experienced as "enough." **The game of the conscious mind is to stay tuned-in to the enoughness of what is now in our lives—no matter what melodrama we may be involved in.** Regardless of whether we are sick or well, employed or unemployed, with a lover or without one, wealthy or poor, we always have enough to enjoy our here and now—unless we are letting our addictions run away with us and destroy our **overall tuning-in** to what we do have now in our lives.

We do not have to put off living—and enjoying. By upleveling our addictions to preferences, and using the Pathways as a guide, we can operate the wonderful mental apparatus that we possess in a way that enables us to genuinely enjoy the here and now in our lives. We can create a succession of "now moments" that are characterized by enjoyment, serenity, energy, love and purpose. Our lives are disturbed by fewer addictive demands. We can celebrate life as a beautiful game in which the payoffs are an ever-increasing love of ourselves and others.

*I take full responsibility here and
now for everything I experience, for
it is my own programming that
creates my actions and also influences
the reactions of people around me.*

8

you create
your world

LET'S LOOK AT WHY ALMOST
everyone alive is creating far less enjoyment from life than
is possible. Almost everyone on this planet lives in a world
of illusion in which the separate-self programming constantly creates the framework of "me vs. other people" or
a self-downing "me vs. myself." This subject-object split is
consistently used by the unskillful mind when processing
incoming sensory information and subtly blending it with
distorted versions of past memories and current addictive
models. We operate our minds under the illusion that the

rational mind functions as a truth-seeking instrument. Actually, it usually operates to select, bias and create concepts that rationalize, justify and try to make us feel "right" about the addictive programmings of the separate-self.

We take a giant step forward in our consciousness growth when we begin to understand the scientific validity of the principle, "I take full responsibility here and now for everything I experience . . . ." Usually our minds lump together "what is" and our experience of "what is." As we previously discussed, "what is" refers to "reality"; **but our experience of "what is" is created by our minds based on our programming.** When we uncritically assume that our experience is totally caused by "what is," and do not see it as a function of our programming, we lay ourselves open to illusion and suffering.

YOUR PROGRAMMING CREATES YOUR EXPERIENCE

What is the difference between "reality" and your experience of what's happening? **What is real—and what is created by your mind?** Let's look at an example. The sun came up this morning. This is "what is"—this is "reality." You are not creating the rotation of the earth, which causes the sun to appear above the horizon and change night into day. This is the physical universe doing its thing.

But your experience of the sunrise is an entirely different matter. YOU CREATE YOUR EXPERIENCE. You can experience it as an awful event and criticize the universe for not giving you several more hours of sleep, or you can view it as a joyous happening full of resplendent hues and colors and the beginning of a beautiful new day. You can greet the sunrise with low energy or with high exuberant energy—or you may just be indifferent to it. You may sleep through it and have no experience of the sunrise.

Whatever is happening, you create your experience—or lack of it. The world is not creating your experience. Your

mind is doing it. When using the addictive separate-self programming, your mind will inevitably create the experience that there's you and there's the sunrise—and the sunrise itself determines your experience. But as you begin to grow in consciousness, you realize that you can always take full responsibility for your experience without blaming yourself or others. The world is not doing it to you. You can only do it to yourself. And this insight opens the way for you to learn to be the creative cause of your experience—instead of staying trapped in robot-like illusions. You can choose the programming you want to live with.

The most accurate way to understand your experience is to view it as a joint phenomenon of the sensory input from outside and inside of you interacting with your addictive and preferential programming, memories, emotions and other aspects of the structure and functioning of your own particular nervous system. There isn't much you can do about controlling the sunrise. But there is a great deal you can do to create an enjoyable experience of the sunrise.

This is why the Fifth Pathway places squarely on your shoulders the full responsibility for your experience. It is up to you to recognize your addictive programmings that make you vulnerable to creating separating experiences. You can then choose to handle your addictions that trigger fear, anger, jealousy, frustration, hatred, irritation or resentment—or to continue to live with what you are now creating.

As long as you let your mind get away with blaming other people (or the outside world) for the unpleasant experiences you create, you will remain stuck in a world of illusion. Your energy to improve your life will take the unfortunate form of beating on the people around you—psychologically or otherwise. You may continually tell yourself that your life would be much "better" if people would act differently. While this may be true, you win some and you lose some. Some people will not act differently. And whether or not they change, feeling angry or uptight doesn't do **you** any good in improving the quality of your experience. You're keeping yourself trapped!

Since you create your own experience, make it easy on yourself! **Work on your own head in addition to trying to shape up the behavior of other people.** It's O.K. to put out for what you want. Go ahead and try to change the outside world. But don't forget to look at your addictive demands when life isn't meeting your models. Build up your skill in handling them.

RESPONSIBILITY WITHOUT BLAME

It's important that you not twist this principle of taking responsibility for your experience by blaming yourself for your fear or anger. It is possible to take full responsibility—without blaming anybody. After all, you are not your programming any more than a stereo set is the record that it plays. You don't blame a stereo set if the record is scratchy. Similarly, it retards your consciousness growth if you blame yourself—**for you will be blaming an innocent person.** Blaming yourself takes your energy away from the inner work you could be doing in learning to handle your addictions.

Much of your programming was put into you when you were too young to understand what the programming of the mind was all about. The words and actions of the people who took care of you in your first few years of life, the experiences you had with your playmates, the things you saw on TV or learned at school—all of these contributed toward giving you the programmings that you now have in your mind. And you don't have to blame the people you've known. They were just acting out the programming they took on.

A lot of the programming you acquired is preferential programming that adds to the richness of your life. But some of it is addictive and each addiction causes you to create upset, unpleasantness and turmoil in your mind. Your addictions are so frequently activated that you are often unhappy. An inventory I have used indicated that many people are carrying over one hundred addictive programmings—and some people have over two hundred! They're like bees buzzing around your head!

You can enormously increase the enjoyment of your life by using the Pathways to handle your addictions or to up-level your addictions to preferences **without any blaming of yourself.** You are your best ally and helpmate on your journey to higher consciousness. **If there is an enemy, it's not you—it is the addictive programming that was put into your biocomputer many years ago.**

The Fifth Pathway thus reminds you that the game is responsibility—not blame. Taking full responsibility and emotionally blaming do not go together. Blaming is addictive; responsibility is preferential. **Blaming perpetuates the separate-self. It keeps you from really taking responsibility.**

HANDLING YOUR ADDICTIONS

If there is an arrow in your heart and you're bleeding to death, it doesn't make much sense to get into a big hassle trying to blame someone for doing it. The important thing is to get the arrow out and heal the wound. Addictive programmings are like wounds or cancers in our minds. Don't worry about where they came from. That's the dead past and it usually won't help you with your addictions.

Concentrate on what's now—the game of using the Pathways to **handle your addictions** and perhaps gradually change your addictive programming into preferential programming. You may consider that you are **handling your addictions** to the degree that:

1. You are aware of your **specific** addictive demand or demands.

2. Your rational mind is no longer blaming yourself or others for the experience you are creating (even

though emotionally you may still feel like blaming).
3. You are using the Pathways to work on your specific addiction or addictions as described in Chapter 16.

These are three criteria that will enable you to determine whether you are **handling your addictions** using the Living Love methodology. When you are doing these three things, you have taken an addiction from the unconscious phase to the awakening phase.

THE WELLSPRINGS OF ACTION

The second part of the Fifth Pathway reminds you to become increasingly aware of how your own programming creates your actions. The things that you feel, think, say and do are not coming out of the blue sky. **Nor are they determined by your free choice as spontaneously as it might seem to you.** They are actually a product of the addictive and preferential programmings in your mind interacting with your incoming stream of sensory data—most of which is handled on unconscious levels.

We often have the illusion that we creatively and spontaneously decide what to do. However, neurological data show that the unconscious part of the mind integrates the incredibly complex incoming information with our various programmings. The vast circuitry of our unconscious mind produces our decisions a fraction of a second before they are projected onto the screen of our consciousness—and we become aware of them! Our minds are handling millions of bits of information every second. The eyes alone send in messages to the brain using about two million nerve fibers. Our unconscious minds sort out and selectively arrange priorities based on our various programmings.

Our programmed priorities thus determine what things are projected onto the screen of our consciousness so that we may become aware of them. The programming of a mother may automatically arouse her from sleep when her baby coughs—while the programming of another person

73

may not select this data to be projected onto the screen of consciousness—and s/he continues sleeping. Because of your programming, you will often pick out the sound of **your** name from a huge babble of talk that is going on at a noisy party, whereas other people will pick out **their** own names from the same jumble of sounds.

As you become more aware of the ways in which your mind operates, you can learn to alter its programming as needed to help your life work better. You will be able to witness many of your various programmings interacting with your memory banks and the marvelous logical-intellectual capacities of your mind. You can watch expectantly for the course of action that your mind wishes to activate. You can observe this process happening in your own mind—somewhat analogous to your putting data into a programmed computer, pushing the button and waiting for the final printout that tells you "the answer." Just as with the computer, you may not be aware of the inner workings of the machinery. But you can be tuned-in to many of the input elements, the preferential and addictive programs, as well as the "printout" that your ego releases to the screen of consciousness for you to notice.

THE WORLD IS YOUR MIRROR

The Fifth Pathway contains three main ideas:

1. Taking full responsibility for your experience.
2. Seeing your actions as flowing from your programming.
3. Taking responsibility for your programming influencing the reactions of people around you.

As you become more aware of how your mind works, you increasingly understand how you create your own experience—and in a large part "create" the more significant human-to-human aspects of the world around you. You do not live in a vacuum. You are surrounded by highly responsive feedback systems known as "human beings."

If I act in angry, hostile ways, the people around me will most likely respond in angry, hostile ways (unless they are operating their consciousness in the unified, rather than separate, mode). If I put out energies of loving and serving the people around me, they will tend to mirror this back to me. When I smile and laugh, the feelings of people around me will tend to rise. When I am moody and depressed, I will tend to create moodiness and depression around me.

The world is thus my mirror. If I don't like what I see in the mirror, as a conscious person I can work to change my own addictive demands to preferences. This increases my ability to radiate love and to flow a caring energy into the world. Blaming the "mirror" (other people) or trying to change the "mirror" (other people) is an unskillful way to respond to the unpleasant images in the "mirror." Working on my own head so that I begin to radiate openness, humor, lightness, love and caring can be guaranteed to improve the images in the "mirror" (the responses of people around me).

When you unconsciously run separate-self programming, you create the illusion of the world as a great big thing out there that constantly threatens you. You have the hopeless point of view that there's not much you can do to change it—you're just a pawn in the grip of circumstances. As the poet A. E. Housman put it, "I, a stranger and afraid / In a world I never made."

As you begin to work on your addictions, you'll discover that you've been creating your own unsatisfactory emotions of fear, frustration and anger. And you've also been triggering the addictions of people around you. Although **their** addictions create **their** experience, **your actions can trigger their addictions.** And you thus play your part in producing the script for the current act in the melodrama of your life.

75

In a very real sense, you even "create" your immediate environment—for you usually have a choice to live in the city or the country, to live in California or in Virginia, to drive a car or to bicycle or walk, to turn on the television or to read a book, and so forth. By your choices of which environment you put your body in, and what you choose to do in that environment once you're in it, you create your world of experience. Again, the world isn't doing it to you; you're doing it to yourself!

So the good news of the Fifth Pathway is that you are a godlike being who creates the world you experience. If you don't like what's happening in your life, the Pathways can point the way to creating far more continuous enjoyment, inner peace and love for yourself and others.

Every time you blame someone else for your experience, or every time you blame yourself for your experience, you are choosing to continue to live in a world of illusion and separateness. To the degree that you see that your addictive programming is the real problem that makes you create unpleasant experiences, you possess the key to begin skillfully creating a more enjoyable experience of your life.

I accept myself completely here and now and consciously experience everything I feel, think, say and do (including my emotion-backed addictions) as a necessary part of my growth into higher consciousness.

9
you're blaming an innocent person

O UR "LAW" OF HIGHER CON-sciousness states, **"Love everyone unconditionally—including yourself"—or especially yourself!** It emphasizes the importance of learning to emotionally accept yourself. **A mind that is critical and judgmental and has a low self-esteem can only offer a shallow acceptance and love to other people.**

We create our perception of others. What our minds select as important about another person is that which fits in with the addictive programmings we use in complimenting ourselves—or downing ourselves. In other words, **what we see in another person is what we are addictively accepting or rejecting in ourselves.** A human being has thousands of other characteristics, but we just rapidly run this data in and out of our awareness (or ignore it) since our minds do not regard these characteristics as important. **Thus our minds recognize as "important" in other people that which we addictively like or don't like (or would like or would not like) in ourselves!**

LEARNING TO LOVE YOURSELF

In our trainings, we begin with the assumption that most of us have some cleanup work to do in learning to accept and love ourselves. When we were children, our parents were often critical and downing in their responses to us. "You're bad" instead of "I don't like what you did just now." "Stupid! Can't you remember what I told you?" instead of "I get tired of telling you this again and again."

When parents are caught in addictions, they issue critical judgments about the child instead of taking responsibility for their own experience as discussed in the last chapter. The form of our language (such as "You are terrible") implies that qualities such as bad, awful, untruthful, stupid, irresponsible, dishonest, messy, ugly, mean, unlovable and incapable are like rocks that are deeply imbedded into the makeup of the child. Parents are often unaware that these are only their own emotional judgments based on their addictions. **They think they are talking about the child. Actually, their own addictive programmings are the immediate, practical cause of their experience.** (Review Chapters 2 and 3 if you don't understand this last statement.)

Of course, children have many addictions that lead them to run off huge amounts of fear, frustration and anger. Parents addictively demand that children avoid screaming and fighting, be cooperative, grateful, and otherwise shape up to meet their models. The child usually picks up the ad-

Sixth Pathway: I accept myself completely here and now and consciously experience everything I feel, think, say and do (including my emotion-backed addictions)
as a necessary part of my growth into higher consciousness.

dictive demands of the parents and then resists by stepping
up his or her own addictive demands even more.

It helps when parents can see their own addictive demands and the child's addictive demands winding up tighter
and tighter—and somehow break the buildup of separateness by working on themselves to bring love and understanding back into their hearts. When parents work only
on the child, constantly making him or her wrong, they will
ignorantly block the development of self-confidence and
love in a growing human being.

Many parents have fallen into this trap of being constantly critical of their children. They do not clearly take
responsibility for creating their own angry or irritable
feelings when the child does certain things (or does not do
certain things). Whatever games they may win by power
tripping the child, **they lose the love game.**

Over a period of years, the subject-object, separate-self
criticalness and conditional love created by your parents
and others in your life probably took a heavy toll in keeping
you from learning to accept and love yourself. And the price
that you may have paid for this unskillful parenting is low
self-esteem and low feelings of self-worth. No matter how
beautifully you live, no matter how much you may "a-
chieve," no matter how lovingly and generously you may
treat your brothers and sisters, **this nagging inner feeling
of low self-worth and low lovability will probably continue until you look at it as only a programming of your
mind—and use the Pathways or other methods to root it
out.**

This may be difficult because this low-esteem programming is usually accompanied by emotional feelings of guilt,
worthlessness, suppression and repression of your feelings,
great self-judgmentalness and self-criticalness—and a desire to hide. Even when you do something really fine, a nagging inner voice that was programmed during childhood
may often say, "I was just lucky that time. I hope people
don't notice how I really am." You may constantly sabotage

79

your experience by telling yourself that you are not beautiful, not capable and not lovable—and that you don't deserve to be happy.

When you are running self-rejection tapes, you may be continuing to use your parents' method of controlling you. Withholding love from yourself and expecting to use it as a reward for when you meet your models does not work because **it is never enough.** No matter how successful you are, your ego-mind will always find some other area in which you need to improve. This power tripping of yourself will not bring you love and inner peace. **There is never a good enough reason for withholding love from anyone— including yourself.**

You may have a core belief that you will be a better person by being sharply critical and judgmental of yourself. It doesn't work that way. **The best context in which to change yourself is to love yourself without that change.**

Something significant begins to happen in the operation of your mind **when you see these self-rejecting tapes as just tapes.** This can increase your insight into the ways in which self-rejecting tapes become self-fulfilling prophecies. Telling yourself that you're incapable can block your ability to learn and practice the life-opening skills offered by the Pathways.

As you work on yourself, you learn that positive tapes, such as "I am beautiful, capable and lovable," can also become self-fulfilling prophecies. For your mind has the ability to create any psychological reality that it is willing to create. The techniques described in this book can gradually help you reprogram these self-rejecting tapes—and develop a loving self-accepting attitude. But it takes lots and lots of skillful inner work on yourself.

A DAILY PRACTICE

The Sixth Pathway can be helpful to you in silencing these inappropriate tapes that your well-meaning but harassed parents (and other people, too) may have helped you to program during the early formative years of your life. It could be particularly beneficial if you also use the reprogramming phrase "I am beautiful, capable and lovable" and alternate this with the Sixth Pathway. In other words, first silently or aloud say the Sixth Pathway, then "I am beautiful, capable and lovable," then repeat the Sixth Pathway, etc.

In our trainings we often use a traffic counter purchased at an office supply store. This gives us the fun of pushing the counter button, and it helps as a reminder when our minds want to distract us. You'll find it easier to consistently and skillfully work on yourself if you have this mechanical counter to play with. Each time you say, "I am beautiful, capable and lovable," push the button; each time you repeat a Pathway, push the counter button again. Continue alternating this reprogramming phrase with the Pathways 500 to 1,000 times per day for the next three months.

The daily practice described above can be a great help in reducing the grip of unconscious (as well as conscious) tapes that exercise such a tyrannical control over the doors of your perception. Always remember that just knowing about these Pathways is only a first step—they need to be used in a practical way to replace the deep-level programs in your mind that are now keeping you from getting the most from your life.

ACCEPTING YOURSELF COMPLETELY

Let's particularly notice the word "completely" in the Sixth Pathway when it says, "I accept myself completely here and now." Emotional acceptance of yourself and of things you say and do can be complete—with patient practice. Emotional acceptance means that you do not waste the energy of your mind and body in rejecting yourself by running judgmental and critical tapes about yourself or your thoughts or actions. It means that your acceptance and love of yourself is unflickering.

You don't have to like everything you do—that is the soap opera. What you accept and love is **you.** Remember, you're not your tapes. To return to the stereo analogy, you accept and love the stereo—and it's O.K. to toss out a bad sounding record. Toss out your addictive programming—not you!

If something does not turn out the way you want it to, **you can experience the situation as offering practice you need to increase your skill in handling similar situations in the future.** In other words, you see it as a richness that lets you develop a higher level of insight in operating your life. You need not use self-rejecting tapes as proof of how terrible you are deep down inside. When you accept yourself completely, you do not have to maintain a phony front, drive yourself to "achieve," or feel self-conscious if people are watching you. The Sixth Pathway, when used as suggested in Chapter 16, can help you stop running those painful self-conscious tapes that keep you from accepting yourself.

Can you **accept yourself emotionally and still try to change** some of your programming? Of course! Emotionally accepting yourself does not keep you from using the Pathways to reprogram certain tapes that you feel are ripping off your happiness. Accepting yourself completely here and now does not mean that you cannot **prefer** to remember names better or to have a more beautiful singing voice or whatever. It simply means that these will just be preferences, not addictions—and that you will not use these models or thoughts to reject yourself or hide yourself. Actually, when you emotionally accept "what is" about yourself, you have a greater ability to change anything you want to.

Self-rejection is actually a beautiful cop-out from taking responsibility for working on yourself. In working on self-acceptance, the crucial game is to love yourself just as much when you don't meet your models of perfection as when you do. Accepting yourself means you do not buy in when your mind judgmentally compares you with others or with models of yourself based on the dead past or the imagined future. It means you don't create a self-deprecating, self-downing experience when others excel in some area. There are thousands of skills that human beings have become adept at. No human being can possibly possess all these skills. There will always be some people who are better and some people who are not as good as you in almost any game in life.

Accepting yourself means that it's O.K. for others to be better than you. You do not have to create your life as a cliff-hanging, competitive event. **There's no way to meet your models of perfection 100% of the time.** You win some and you lose some. That's the way it is for everybody.

In the melodrama of your life, you do not have to play the part of someone else you admire. You can admire others and still just play your own part. Tell your mind that it doesn't need to run these self-rejecting tapes by comparing yourself with others. You don't have to be best in everything—or anything. Running such a comparison perpetuates your moment-to-moment creation of the separate-self. Your skill in any game doesn't make you more lovable, nor does your lack of skill make you unlovable. Such self-conscious thoughts are simply part of your addictive programming.

You can let yourself experience that you are a perfect you. You always have been. You are already beautiful, capable and lovable. You can enjoy your life instead of driving yourself. You can learn to handle the tapes that say you have to be different from the way you are **right this minute** in order to be lovable. Before you can really accept and enjoy the love others feel for you, you must feel love for yourself.

CONSCIOUSLY EXPERIENCING

The Sixth Pathway advises us to "consciously experience everything...." Most people are unconsciously experiencing their lives—and they have lots of addictive snarls and unhappiness to prove it. In the last chapter we discussed **handling your addictions,** which means you are **beginning to "consciously experience" your life in an addictive area.** Let's review the three ways that indicate the degree to which you are handling your addictions. To begin consciously experiencing "what is" in an area in which you were previously "unconscious," step by step you begin to (1) increasingly notice your specific addictive demand, (2) take intellectual responsibility for creating your experience (even though you still feel like blaming) and (3) use the Pathways to work on your addictive demands. Thus, when you're handling your addictions, on one hand you're still caught up emotionally, and on the other hand you are no longer running off your addictive tapes "unconsciously." When you have a separating emotional feeling, you are aware of the part your addictive programming plays in triggering it. You are beginning to awaken.

When you become consciously aware of your desire systems **as desire systems,** you open the door for replacing addictive tapes that are causing problems in your life. These include addictive security, sensation and power tapes that the mind uses to create a constant experience of threat— that life is a battle instead of a beautiful cooperative game that we can all play together. The world can be offering us its cornucopia of treasures, and we can fail to even notice them if our addictive programs are tormenting our minds and bodies.

SELF-CONSCIOUSNESS

Self-consciousness is an addictive programming of the separate-self. In learning to accept ourselves completely, it is helpful to get a feeling of how self-consciousness can distort the operation of the mind. When we were a few months old and just beginning to learn to walk, we probably had hundreds of painful sprawls ahead of us. No baby can be crawling one day and stand up erect the next day and walk without falling. Learning to walk is a gradual process that is accomplished over a period of time.

However, at nine months we did not have an addictive model that we should be able to walk perfectly. We were able to experience and practice this skill in a simple and consistent way. We fell time and time again, **but we were not self-conscious when we fell.** Our ego-minds at nine months did not say, "You're awful; you'll never learn to walk." Even though we did not like falling, our minds did not have a facility with concepts that enabled us to reject ourselves because we could not walk as well as two-year olds. So we just kept falling and falling and learning and learning, and there came a day when we were pretty good at walking.

Experiencing life day by day gives your mind the mes-sages it needs to reprogram what you need to learn. But we usually don't let our minds consciously experience our lives. Instead, we self-consciously and critically watch our-selves—instantly ready to compare and reject ourselves. It's like always walking on eggs. This self-consciousness is a distraction to the mind. It is not only unpleasant but ac-tually slows down our naturally learning the lessons of life.

A critical self-consciousness that triggers guilt, shame and embarrassment often takes the fun out of life. It is inter-esting to note that animals are usually not self-conscious. They are conscious, but not self-conscious. Similarly, we would enjoy our lives more if our minds no longer ener-gized addictive, self-conscious programmings to trigger separating emotions of guilt, shame and embarrassment.

A first step is to have the insight that what you do or say (or how people respond to you) **does not make you feel these self-conscious emotions.** People do what they do, of course, but it is **your addictive tapes** in your head that are

85

the **immediate, practical cause** of your feelings of guilt, shame, embarrassment, humiliation, self-rejection, etc. Addictions are always the problem!

ADDICTIONS ABOUT ADDICTIONS

As you increasingly use the Pathways, you may develop an addiction to not have any addictions. If consciously used, this overarching addiction may be helpful to flow your energy into working on your other addictions. But since this is still an addiction, it can keep you from creating an enjoyable experience in your life. If you succeed in rooting out most of your addictions from an addictive space, you may then tend to be addictively critical of other people who have not upleveled many of their addictions. Being addicted to not having addictions makes you impatient with yourself and your growth and keeps you from enjoying your life.

You can **prefer** to work on your addictions, and to uplevel them to preferences. Like the common cold, addictions are a fact of life. Everybody has them. And the best way to work on your addictions—including addictions about how you should be—is not to reject your addictions but to accept them emotionally. Then use the Pathways to handle them and eventually uplevel many of them to preferences.

LIFE IS A TRAINING LABORATORY

The last part of the Sixth Pathway suggests that you experience everything you feel, think, say and do (including your emotion-backed addictions) "as a necessary part of my growth into higher consciousness." Your soap opera may be viewed as a testing and training laboratory for the mind. The tapes you now have in your head are a part of your here-and-now mental equipment. So what do you do about them?

You can't just think about a tape and tell whether it is addictive or preferential. You obviously have to run your tapes in life situations to check them out. Your life constantly puts you in situations in which you're not getting what you want. And by your gut-level emotional reactions, you quickly know whether you have an addiction—or just a preference. So what you create in your life is a necessary part of your growth. How can you grow except by experiencing what you experience—and hopefully learning the lessons life is offering you? It boils down to whether you're going to work on yourself and use the pains of daily life to gain more insight into how to live your life more skillfully. Or are you going to deny this experience, reject yourself, criticize the world and let the separate-self keep you trapped in a world of addictions, separateness, alienation and low levels of enjoyment?

Even if you don't learn the lessons, you are still entitled to accept yourself and see this resistance as a necessary part of your growth into higher consciousness.

Let the Sixth Pathway help you realize that you can love yourself unconditionally even when you feel you've made mistakes that seem to create "problems" for yourself or other people. It simply means that your mind is living out its programming and **thereby has a chance to shape itself up to serve you better.** Every mistake you make gives you the opportunity to increase your level of skill in handling life situations. **Accepting yourself completely simply means that you are willing to let yourself be a human being on the journey toward greater awareness.**

Accepting yourself means that you are willing to say to yourself and to the world, "Yes! Life has given me a teaching in this situation. I'll learn something that I did not fully understand before. I am thereby richer." Instead of self-rejecting and downgrading yourself in certain life situations, you can tune-in to the perfection of how your life is giving you experiences that increase your ability to play the game of life—and feel at home in the world.

PART IV

Interacting With Others

*I open myself genuinely to all people
by being willing to fully communicate
my deepest feelings, since hiding in
any degree keeps me stuck in my
illusion of separateness from other people.*

10

no more
phony front

THE SEVENTH PATHWAY OFFERS
you one of the quickest ways to feel close to people and to love
them: "I open myself genuinely to all people by being willing to fully communicate my deepest feelings . . . ." You
may be concerned that openness could alienate your friends,
since many of your deepest feelings are anger, fear, irritation, resentment, etc. You may hesitate to fully communicate
your deepest feelings because you tell yourself you don't
want to lay your stuff on other people. And if you were
completely open with other people, you'd have to deal with

your feelings of embarrassment or humiliation. So you are busy hiding the things you'd rather not talk about.

But you're keeping yourself trapped. You're not creating the love and aliveness you could be enjoying. Every persistent, separating feeling that your mind hides from the people in your life acts like a logjam in disturbing the flow of living and loving together.

The key is to avoid blaming another person (or yourself) for your separating feelings. Just take responsibility for them as explained in the Fifth Pathway—and express them:

"I am constantly afraid because I addictively demand that you like me."

"I frustrate myself when I addictively demand that you not keep leaving dishes in the sink."

"I make myself feel separate from you because I addictively demand that you not have the wart on your cheek."

"I make myself feel resentful when I addictively demand you not waste money."

"I'm worried because I am addictively demanding you find me sexually attractive."

First notice your addictive demands and work on them using the Pathways as described in Chapter 16. Then, and this is vital, **communicate to the person involved exactly what you've been working on.** Don't take responsibility for his/her experience. S/he will have to handle whatever addictions you help him or her get in touch with. (Remember, **you** can't make other people angry; you can trigger their addictive programming, and **they** may make themselves angry.) The longer you hide your feelings, the more you'll make yourself feel separate with that person. The longer you build the wall of separateness, the harder it will be to tear it down.

Work on yourself to accept and love people unconditionally —no matter how they respond to you. You don't have to like what people say—for we are not our words. You work on yourself to compassionately remember that people are just running off their addictive programming.

YOU ARE NOT THE TARGET

Laura Huxley reminds us, "You are not the target." Even though aimed at you, you needn't take other people's reactions **personally.** Your addictions probably make you emotionally snap like a tight rubberband when someone shows disapproval of you. **Such vulnerability makes you like a walking bomb—ready to explode or go to pieces whenever someone touches your addictive fuses.** Can you imagine how good it would feel at these times to "stay conscious" and not make yourself afraid or angry when people direct anger or criticism toward you?

During the remaining years of your life, probably everyone you know will sooner or later criticize you or get annoyed or angry at you—unless they're terribly repressed. Would you like to be able to handle your addiction that no one ever criticize you? Or do you want to keep on quaking or churning inside when someone comes on heavy to you? If you want to stay afloat when addictive storms are blowing, you'll have to begin handling your **unrealistic addictive demand** that you not be occasionally buffeted by criticism or anger from the people around you.

THE WILLINGNESS TO COMMUNICATE

The Seventh Pathway suggests that you be **willing** to communicate your deepest feelings. Obviously no one has the time to communicate his or her deepest feelings about everything all the time to everyone. And your ego can use this fact to do a lot of hiding. **The fastest growth occurs when you turn up your courage to communicate your deepest feelings in the situations in which you most want to hide.** You always know deep inside you when things are getting wound up emotionally and it's time for you to "break the ice."

As you live with the Seventh Pathway, you become increasingly aware of the tapes running in your mind which your separate-self doesn't really want to communicate to other people. These are the thoughts and feelings that your separate-self tells you to hide because they're just too confronting, too yucky and too nasty—and would put you in a bad light.

It's only your separate-self that they threaten. **To energize your unified-self, these are exactly the things you need to share.** Hiding your addictive stuff makes it **seem both important and real—and you lose.**

To break through the barriers of separateness, you'll have to talk about what you'd rather hide. Sharing pushes you to face your thoughts and feelings. It is amazing how such confrontation de-energizes them, whereas hiding intensifies them.

Be sure to take responsibility for your blaming, judgmental thoughts as creations of your addictive demands. Don't let your mind get away with insinuating that it's providing you with an objective, accurate description of anything "real" in the world. Notice how your mind uses hiding to "build a case" and make your illusions of separateness seem "real."

Hiding is the main way in which your mind continues to hold on to the activity of the separate-self. Please note that your separate-self is not a solid entity, structure or organ inside of you. **It is simply a functional activity of your mind that you create moment by moment.** When you stop hiding your innermost thoughts and make it O.K. to be where you are, and to express genuinely what you are creating inside, you will become more aware of this separate-self activity of the mind. And you'll want to stop creating this separate-self as you begin to see what it does to limit the love and harmony in your life.

DEEPER LEVELS OF OPENNESS

The Seventh Pathway can inspire you to let go of trying to make your life work by being phony. It means that you no longer see yourself as so different from other people that you can't "let it all hang out." You realize that the intense need for privacy that you have created in the past is only a strategy of your mind to maintain your separate-self programming.

As you open yourself more and more to people and to life, you will find that you increasingly accept all of your feelings. And when you begin to accept yourself more deeply as suggested by the Sixth Pathway, you find that you can share all of your "stuff" with other people. You will no longer let your separate-self programmings control you by creating embarrassment or shame—and thus make you feel that you have to hide some things. Your life becomes an open game of "me in the world"—instead of a secret game of "me vs. the world."

Let's face it. You often don't express your feelings of anger, resentment and fear because you want to be nice and polite. But how helpful is all this politeness anyway? Does it really bring you closer to your friends and your family? When you close off a part of your thoughts to another person, you make them a separate "object"—you keep yourself from perceiving him or her as "us." Your hiding makes you experience people as "him," "her" or "them." And remember, **it's how you operate your mind that determines whether another person is one of "them" or one of "us."** You tend to blame their actions for the separateness you experience. But your addictive demands that lead you to shut down your deeper levels of inner honesty always create your feelings of separateness and alienation. And the gulf is usually widened when others simultaneously trigger their addictions and stop communicating honestly, too.

Living Love is nourished by living truth when you open yourself genuinely by being willing to fully communicate your deepest feelings. Life is a river of energy. You dam up the flow when you fail to share what your mind is creating.

95

You trap yourself and you may trap others in the labyrinths of separateness you are creating. You make your fear and resentment "real" and "important" when you lock it up inside you. Your mind acts as a magician that creates the "illusion of separateness."

Sometimes there will be turmoil when we share the garbage our minds have created! But life can be more fun when we face it honestly and wade through the garbage together **so that we don't have to live with it any more.** Sharing openly helps us let go of the "illusion of separateness" created by our addictive tapes. And we'll live happier and longer when we handle our addictive demands that can bring on high blood pressure, create ulcers, destroy our aliveness, and even hasten our deaths.

There may come a day when you realize that the most freeing thing that could happen would be for all of your innermost thoughts to be printed on the front page of the morning newspaper! Many of your separate-self games would be instantly blown by this openness. It would feel good to stand tall and feel free around everyone—no need to try to hide anything for everyone knows "the worst" about you. And you could experience that **there is nothing special about your "worst."** We are all busy maintaining this separate-self—and at the same time longing for a cooperative, loving life. The two don't work together. The cooperative, loving life is an automatic consequence of the unified-self.

All of your separate-self emotion-backed addictions make you vulnerable to throwing people out of your heart—and keep the real you in hiding. The more you know about how the mind energizes addictions, the more effectively you can learn to handle them. Some of our addictions are accompanied by strong emotions and are very obvious to us. Others are subtle and mainly create resisting or clinging thoughts. There is a continuum from the strongest, violent addictive emotions all the way down to the fleeting "me-vs.-them" thoughts without separating emotions.

It is important that we learn to fully communicate the entire spectrum of addictive demands. It's easy to be aware of the need to handle addictions that cause us to act out or emote out a drama of separateness—for these obviously cause a lot of turmoil in our lives. But to enter into the highest levels of enjoying life, it is necessary for us to also share our addictive demands that spawn non-emotional but still separating thought forms. So let's examine how addictions, like horseradish, come in three strengths—hot, warm and mild.

ACTING OUT, EMOTING OUT AND THINKING OUT

There are three levels of addictive strength: acting out, emoting out and thinking out. When you are **acting out** an addiction, your behavior is sufficiently altered so that it could be picked up by a sound-camera. Other people can tell what's going on in your head by your speech, the tone of your voice and your actions. Addictively striking someone is an obvious example of acting out. If you're addictively demanding that you not have to wash dishes, acting out could involve setting the dishes down angrily. Or you could act out by "forgetting" to wash dishes. Acting out also includes subtler behavior, such as quietly sulking or not approaching someone for fear of rejection. If a camera were on you long enough, it could pick up the acting out of your withdrawal.

To stop emoting out or thinking out may require the kind of inner work on your addictive demands that we are describing in this book. By observing how your mind works, you will notice that you can usually choose in each life situation whether to act out or not! You cannot, however, stop emoting out or thinking out through an act of will. One way to find out if you are ready for rapid consciousness growth is to ask yourself if you want to stop acting out your addictive demands—and then honestly face whether you will work on yourself to learn **to handle** the separating emotions and thoughts that arise in your mind. (You may wish to review the three things you must be doing to handle your addictions. See the section on "Handling Your Addictions" in Chapter 8.)

When you are simply **emoting out** an addiction, although you're experiencing a separating emotion, it is not affecting your outward behavior—just your inner experience. You may have physical tension somewhere in your body. If you're carrying an addiction that you not be expected to wash dishes, emoting out could take the form of actually washing the dishes but feeling resentful and irritated inside.

When you are acting out an addiction, you will automatically be emoting out and thinking out. When you're emoting out, you will automatically be thinking out an addictive demand. But when the addictive strength has been decreased to the thinking-out level, you will no longer be either acting out or emoting out.

When you are only **thinking out** an addiction, the addictive strength has been greatly diminished. There is a genuine absence of any physical sensation or separating emotion. You are not suppressing. But your mind is disturbed or concerned. Your consciousness is dominated by what you experience as a "problem." In the thinking-out phase of an addictive demand to avoid dishwashing, you can flow energy into washing dishes but your mind will most likely run such tapes as, "I should be doing other things," "Where did all these dishes come from?" "I wonder how much an automatic dishwasher would cost," etc.

Such tapes can run from a preferential space, too. But there is a difference between an addiction at thinking-out strength and a preference. When it's a preference, your mind does not experience having a "serious problem"; you can lightly play the games of life. When it's an addiction, the tapes keep repeating over and over, and in varying degrees they keep you from enjoying your here and now. If you continue to work on your subtle addictive desires in the thinking-out stage of an addiction, it will most likely be upleveled to a preference—sooner or later. To make it sooner, it is many times more effective to openly share all of your addictive demands with other people regardless of whether the addictions are in the acting-out, emoting-out or thinking-out strength.

THE ILLUSION OF SEPARATENESS

One of the most important parts of the Seventh Pathway is the phrase "illusion of separateness." The separate-self constantly gives us the impression that separateness is normal, correct and the way things are, and that life is a struggle against our environment. We manage to create a self-fulfilling prophecy from this "illusion of separateness." If we say and do things that are motivated by our "illusion of separateness," we will continually create a life of conflict.

It's easy to create the jungle consciousness. We "wind tight" the addictive situations in our lives so as to create an unbroken experience of the separate-self. But this is always an "illusion" in the sense that it is not the way life is—we are creating an apparently solid separate-self by continuously running our addictive programming. You can use a life situation, such as being fired from your job as described in Chapter 7, to run off the separate-self programming in which you create **a personal battle** between you and another person.

Your mind always has the choice to activate the unified-self programming. For example, you can have a panoramic perspective of yourself playing the worker role and someone else playing the boss role. By seeing these roles **as roles,** you can free yourself from **identifying** with being a worker. For behind all the roles—**here we are**—each of us—**a beautiful, perfect essence of humanity.**

All of our roles are simply parts we are playing in the melodrama of life. Just as an actor on stage can play his or her role without coming under the delusion that s/he is the character portrayed in the role, so can we play our various roles without identifying with the roles—boss, worker, young person, old person, male, female, father, mother, daughter, son, happy person, depressed person, smart person, dumb person, lawyer, salesperson, farmer and so forth. We can play them in a conscious way—**and not confuse our roles with our essence.** When we identify with our essence—our Conscious-awareness—we can consciously observe ourselves playing the games of life.

SEPARATE-SELF PROGRAMS

As we discussed in Chapter 6, the separate-self programs were developed by our ancestors millions of years ago for survival in the jungle. Most animals have to compete with other animals for food and mates. They have natural predators who would like to eat them for supper tonight. The programs of fight or flight or hiding must be very strong and automatic for animals to survive in the ever-present competition and dangers of the jungle.

The ten billion cortical cells in our brains that give us the capacity to build such excellent "me-vs.-them" cases can also **enable us to free ourselves from this separate-self way of operating our minds.** Far more effective methods are now available to us through the activation of the unified-self programming. But most of us are not aware of this yet. We're still trying to make our lives work using the outmoded jungle techniques of operating our minds. **Unfortunately, few of us understand that no other person, however filled with hate, can hurt us and destroy our enjoyment of life as much as we are now doing to ourselves by our daily runoff of our separate-self addictive demands.** Let's suppose that your supervisor notices that you are fifteen minutes late for work and she calls you to her office and really "lets you have it" with her separate-self tapes. If you process this melodrama through your separate-self programming, your mind will come up with thought forms such as "The bitch. She doesn't understand. The traffic was heavy this morning and there was nothing I could do. She doesn't like me and I don't like her. I'll get even with her."

Now let's suppose you have worked on yourself using the Pathways. You have increased your skill so that you can handle this type of situation through your unified-self programming. Instead of the above separate-self thoughts, your mind could come up with such thought forms as, "She's really making herself upset over this matter. I guess if I were supervisor and had to fight today's rising costs of running a business, I would be concerned when people don't arrive on time. **All appearances to the contrary, there is nothing personal in any of this.** She is just running off her 'boss role' as she sees it. My love and compassionate understanding are large enough to cover this life situation."

Instead of angry resistance or obsequious honey-coating, your unified-self reply to your supervisor might go something like this: "I hear what you're saying. I was fifteen minutes late, and I'll try to allow more time for traffic jams in the future. I know we have a lot of worries coping with rising costs. I want to cooperate by getting to work on time. I totally understand what you're telling me and I appreciate your taking the time to do it."

When you use the unified-self programming instead of your separate-self tapes, you won't have to make yourself upset all day long, you can love yourself and the supervisor, **and you may come out of the melodrama with your supervisor actually liking you more because you understand her problems.** You keep this insignificant happening from being magnified into a mountain of separateness, alienation and revenge. And you can do it without repressing your anger, fear or frustration.

FIVE STEPS TOWARD THE UNIFIED-SELF

So how do you begin to energize your unified-self? There's no button you can push that will remove separate-self programming and replace it with unified-self programming. You begin by clearly seeing the effects of these two different types of programming in your life. You may notice that the jungle-type separate-self programming **operates rapidly and automatically.** We've had millions of years of practice with this type of programming. It got us through eons in the jungle. But in this nuclear age, it may not get us through the next hundred years!

Here are five steps for working on yourself to go beyond the illusion of separateness: First, develop a clear understanding of the disadvantages and dangers of the separate-self and the great benefits to be had from unified-self programming. Second, resolve to practice with the Pathways until they can be relied upon to work automatically.

The third step is to emotionally accept yourself when you trigger fear, frustration or anger. By making it O.K. to feel them, you don't down yourself, criticize yourself, judge yourself or in any way blame yourself. You simply view yourself as a pioneer in the long journey of increasing consciousness. We started millions of years ago. No doubt we will not finish by tomorrow. Be patient and give yourself time.

But work with yourself for it will not happen without **a deep dedication** to doing this inner work. Always be sure that you're **not rejecting yourself.** You're working to change only the separate-self programs of your mind that are holding you back from getting the most from your life.

The fourth step is to consciously watch your mind run off the addictive separate-self programs. Note that every time you have an addictive demand and are feeling angry, afraid, irritated, jealous or upset in any way, you are running a separate-self program. Observe how your addictive demands work as a team to create what we call the "separate-self." These insights are needed to creatively uplevel the functioning of your mind so that you are **handling your addictions.**

The fifth step is to do a daily mental practice that enables you to accomplish this inner work. Simple techniques for using the Pathways as a mental tool are described in Chapters 9 and 16. Always keep in mind that the separate-self will be created less and less as you uplevel addictions to preferences. The whole game boils down to demanding less —and loving more!

To summarize the five steps:

1. Understand the rip-offs of the separate-self and the advantages of the unified-self.

2. Resolve to do something about it.

3. Accept and love yourself even when you continue to create separating emotions.

4. Begin to observe your mind in action so that you see how your addictions create your experience of the separate-self.

5. Keep using the Pathways in a daily practice until you get the results you want.

YOU'RE NOT A MIND READER

Your inner work will be accelerated if you learn to deeply question (and even mistrust) any thoughts you have **about what's going on in someone else's head. THIS APPLIES 1000% IF YOU ARE FEELING SEPARATE!** Your perceptions, hunches and inferences will seem absolutely correct to you, but they are invariably misleading in one way or another when you are upset. Your inferences about what another person is creating in his or her head are based on what you think you would be thinking if you were in his or her place. But this is only a guess—**no matter how clear and final your mind may declare it.**

If you have multiple addictions with someone and have "built a case" against him or her, there is no possibility that you can stay sensitively tuned-in to this person as he or she lives with a complex life situation. Your addictions make you respond to a fictitious, rock-like set of concepts in your head that you think describe the person.

At this point, it is important to really open yourself genuinely—and deeply communicate to him or her everything you are telling yourself. And you may need to continue to communicate over and over again for many days until you can hear the other person from a unified-self space. **Don't let your impatience keep you from working with a knotty situation.** This is life—and running away or using force may not be the wisest way of handling it. You won't know the best way until you've repeatedly opened yourself to the other person.

Don't demand that someone work on himself or herself. Don't try to make a fair exchange: "I'll be up front if you open up too." **You just do it.** The love and enjoyment that you can eventually create **when you work on yourself** is worth anything you have to go through. The road to love may be bumpy—but it's better than the back alleys we trap ourselves in when we don't fully communicate our deepest feelings—and thereby create and live in separate "worlds" apart.

Your effectiveness in truly communicating will be in direct proportion to your ability to share your deepest feelings instead of silently using your mind to convict the other person of being wrong and get yourself proven right. In spite of any strong emotions that you may have to the contrary, feeling threatened and separate in your heart is always an illusion created by your addictive demands. From the mountaintop perspective, everything other people say and do can be seen by your unified-self as only programs

Seventh Pathway: I open myself genuinely to all people by being willing to fully communicate my deepest feelings, since hiding in any degree keeps me stuck
in my illusion of separateness from other people.

of their minds—however addictive. And people can change
their mental programs . . . .

THE GAMES OF LIFE

From this panoramic vantage point we can get an overall
view of the games of life—as games. We can see life consciously as a melodrama that we are acting out. We can see
that our lives are inextricably interwoven with the lives of
all of our brothers and sisters on this entire planet—socially,
politically, economically, ecologically and otherwise.

We are one world—functioning as a whole. Our separate-
selves have carved up the world into separate territories—
separate countries, separate cities, separate "ownerships"
such as "my business," "my land," "my home," "my friend,"
"my lover"—but none of this is really "mine." It's all "ours"
—a part of the cornucopia of the universe.

The welfare of each of us is interwoven in many, many
ways with the welfare of all of us. We are not as separate as
we assume. A virus carried by someone in Hong Kong
yesterday could under certain circumstances be transmitted
to your body today and make you sick. The political games
of any people on this planet can involve your pocketbook, if
not your life—living as we do in an arsenal of nuclear weapons and biological warfare capability.

We can view the four billion people on this earth as
constant radiators of varying mixtures of hate, separateness and alienation—and also of love, cooperativeness and
happiness. **The mental health of the planet is represented
by the ratio between separateness and cooperative unity.**
Anything that adds to our separateness creates suffering.
Anything that adds to acceptance, love and unity helps us
create happy, enjoyable and fulfilling lives.

If you wish to play the most effective role in improving
your world, as well as your own personal experience of life,
the game is to work on yourself. You work on reducing

your addictions and increasing your love. There is no legislature that can effectively pass a law requiring people to love one another. It's up to each individual to break through his or her own illusions of separateness, and then join together with all brothers and sisters everywhere to eliminate alienation and separateness—and let the planet roll with love.

I feel with loving compassion the problems of others without getting caught up emotionally in their predicaments that are offering them messages they need for their growth.

11

don't buy in

THE EIGHTH PATHWAY HELPS us balance the "head" and the "heart." It begins, "I feel with loving compassion." To feel with compassion means that we understand what someone is going through because we have experienced something similar. This is **not pity or sympathy,** which may mean, "I bleed because you bleed." It is more like **empathy,** which means that my heart feelings and acceptance of myself enable me to be with you and experience you—without making myself upset.

The Eighth Pathway suggests that we let ourselves be with the problems of other people "without getting caught up emotionally in their predicaments that are offering them messages they need for their growth." This has many subtle aspects. Let's explore them together.

Suppose I bought a new car for cash. In the excitement of taking delivery on it, I decided to postpone getting collision and liability insurance until the next day. Let's further suppose that evening a drunk driver without insurance smashed into me. This totaled my car and put me in the hospital.

There are three broad avenues through which you, my best friend, can relate to me and my predicament. Your perceptions and attitudes may largely be determined by your "head" or your "heart"—or by the combined wisdom of your "head" and your "heart." "Head" and "heart" are both experiences that come from the programmings in our minds. Let's look at how each of these three approaches enables you to create a different experience of this situation. Which of the three approaches offers you the most satisfactory inner experience? Which will I find most helpful? Which is the most deeply loving and caring way to relate to me with my ruined car and my subsequent hospitalization? For each of the three approaches described below, we have set up just one of numerous possible ways each scene could be played out.

APPROACH NO. 1: THE "ALL HEAD" APPROACH

Let's suppose you use the "all head" approach. You will have no trouble seeing that life is offering me messages I need for my growth. If you respond to me in this situation by primarily using your logical intellect, you may tell yourself that I was an idiot to drive the car without proper insurance, and that the excitement of the new car made me respond like a child with a new toy who is heedless to adult responsibilities. You may imply that I deserve exactly what

I got. You might not lay this on me that heavily as I lie in traction in my hospital bed, but this is what you could be telling yourself inside. And if this is your inner experience, I may pick it up through the tones in your voice and your body language.

And if I were to argue that my predicament was obviously due to the drunk driver, you might agree that the legal responsibility for the traffic accident is on the other driver. But you may correctly point out that my failure to take out insurance has resulted in the loss of the car and in hospital bills that I will have to pay off over a period of years. You may feel that if I had been a little more attentive and had been driving defensively, I might have avoided the accident. I'll feel that you don't really understand the situation, and that you're not really my friend because you're blaming me for something that any court would agree was not my fault.

If you constantly use only this rational-logical-intellectual approach to life, your friends will find you cold and not understanding, and you'll be the last person they will want to be with when they are in trouble. If I've been criticizing and blaming myself for the predicament I'm in, your visit will trigger my self-rejecting addictions even more. Regardless of any inner feelings of compassion that you may have, in the "all head" approach your rational mind will dominate your basic perceptions. The things you say may be experienced by people as heartless, non-loving and non-caring. You will be "buying into" my predicament via the "all head" route!

APPROACH NO. 2: THE "ALL HEART" APPROACH

Let's suppose the programming of your mind is such that it "buys in" emotionally via the "all heart" approach. Here's one scenario of how this might run. When you visit me in the hospital, you may create an inner experience that a terrible thing has happened to me. You may confirm my illusion that I am in really deep trouble because of this crazy drunk driver. You may be worried about the money that I lost on my car and about my health and whether I'll be O.K. when I leave the hospital. And those bills! You may be concerned about whether I will lose my job because I am missing so much time at work.

Your sympathy for my predicament may encourage my mind to crystallize my addictive anger into a hatred of the intoxicated driver who "should be put in jail and kept there." Although you may try to "cheer me up," we will remain preoccupied with the "great tragedy" that has happened in my life, the unjustness of it all and what an unpredictable and treacherous world we live in. I will probably create the experience that you are my real friend who "stands by me" when I am in trouble.

We may thus develop a mutual consensus of illusions based on looking at only a part of the situation—and not seeing it as a whole. My separate-self can receive ego satisfaction from your visiting me in the hospital and pouring out all of your heartfelt sympathy—and blaming of the other driver. When you are with me in the hospital room, there may be a "juice" that flows between us that temporarily feels good, for it validates my separate-self.

But once you leave, I may drop back into an experience of being trapped by life—hopeless and helpless. Your visits may even help me solidify my feelings of anger, resentment, cynicism and separateness. I may crystallize the illusion of my life as a battle of "me" versus the "world," and create a threatening fear of losing the battle.

In addition to helping me keep myself trapped in separating illusions, your "all heart" approach may not be pleasant to you. You may find that the worry you are addictively creating over my predicament is just too much to carry. I may get myself in the ambivalent position of both wanting you to visit me for the validation you give me and my illusions, and at the same time not wanting you to visit because

I don't want to be responsible for putting all this "burden" on you. This soap opera we are creating between us is characterized **by my taking responsibility for your experience and by your "buying into" my predicament.**

If you were to have a choice to "buy in" via the "head" or the "heart," choose the heart. The bias of the heart is more unifying than the bias of the head. But there is an even higher synthesis that can help your life work better.

APPROACH NO. 3: THE WISDOM OF HEAD AND HEART

Getting the most from life requires a balance of head and heart. **It means not "buying in" emotionally either by the "head" route or the "heart" route.** This integrated approach enables us to find greater enjoyment in our experience of life together. And it is more helpful to each of us.

Now let's look at one form of what it might be like if you operate your nervous system in a way that integrates the perspective of your head and the perspective of your heart—without buying in. In this situation involving my collision, you can be completely aware of all of the tapes that the rational mind and logical intellect can run. But you will not emotionally buy into the critical, judgmental tapes that blame me for not taking out insurance and not driving defensively—although you will see me as responsible for these aspects of the situation.

You know that these are lessons life is offering me. You can even discuss these things in an accepting nonjudgmental way that honors and appreciates the value of the life experiences that we create. You may **empathize** with all of my suffering and tragedy. But you won't trigger pity in yourself, although you can still feel my predicament in compassionate, human terms as though it were your own.

In other words, **you may simultaneously have an awareness of both head and heart tapes.** When you don't emotionally buy in, you can blend them in an intuitive way that comes out as a higher wisdom—and hence qualitatively quite different from either the "head" or "heart" approach when experienced by itself. Instead of concentrating on one aspect of this situation, your experience will be characterized **by a clear seeing of the overall balance of many aspects of my collision and its effect on my life.**

I may feel that you are interested in hearing everything I have to share without buying in, even if I am angry at the drunk driver or am blaming myself. And although I can feel your deep interest, I don't feel that you are joining me in my anger toward the drunk driver. Without your pointing it out in so many words, you are helping me realize that what I am categorizing as a "drunk driver" is another human being like you and me whose programming unfortunately led him into this soap opera.

I may begin to see myself and others as evolving processes (and not just a rock-like set of attributes such as "good" and "bad"). I can also see that this collision is giving the other driver messages that hopefully he may be prepared to hear. Thus without any intellectual analysis, you may create a psychological space in which I can view myself and another person with understanding, compassion and love.

You have the feeling that when you come to see me, you are not just visiting an injured person in the hospital. I feel that you are genuinely enjoying being with me as a human being. You notice that I happen to be playing the orthopedic patient role in the soap opera of life—and you don't act like it's such a big deal. Because you can hear about my physical itches, aches and pains without buying in, you give me the feeling that they are not so all-important. So I don't have to continue to magnify them in my experience. The insight may dawn on me that being bedridden and in a cast is just another form of life. Because you do not emotionally resist my situation, I can begin to let go of my own emotional resistance to what's happening now in my life.

By your refusal to create the illusion that I am caught in a terrible tragedy, you are helping me get a better perspective on all of this. Although right now the hospital is big in my experience, your quiet acceptance helps me see it from a panoramic point of view. I may begin to look at it as only a short interlude in the long span of my life. Since I will probably be out of the hospital in a few weeks, I don't need to keep running all those "poor me" tapes that give more importance to this part of my life than it deserves from a balanced perspective.

HEIGHTENED ENJOYMENT

I see you as creating a turned-on experience when you visit me. In addition to enjoying being with me, you notice the flowers in my room, and you respond with aliveness to the staff as they come and go. And you seem to be appreciating the beauty of now—rather than focusing in a critical way on the color of the walls, the rules of the hospital, etc. In other words, you are enjoying what's enjoyable. That helps me to experience the fact that there are always things (even in the hospital room) that I could enjoy (Fourth Pathway).

I thus find that even when you leave, I may continue experiencing a high feeling that lasts until I run my next addictive tape that makes me reject myself, the other driver, the accident, the hospital room, the nurses, the doctors and my bodily experience of being in a cast. And the more you visit me, the more I begin to realize that I am creating my experience (Fifth Pathway). The world is not doing it to me.

I can see that if I upleveled my addictive demands into preferences, I could actually enjoy being in the hospital, even while I am doing everything possible to get well so that I can leave. I might also notice that my body feels much better and seems to heal more rapidly when I am not addictively resisting being in a hospital. When I let myself relax and enjoy what's here and now, my mind does not push the buttons of depression, fear or anger with all of their psychosomatic runoff.

Your nonjudgmental attitude toward my not taking out insurance and driving more carefully is helping me accept my entire soap opera—for this is "what is" in my life **right here and right now.** If I emotionally reject what's now in my life, I waste the energy that I could more effectively put into changing what's changeable—and enjoying my life in the meanwhile. I don't have to blame myself. I can simply see this as a part of my growth in learning to live my life more consciously.

Using the Sixth Pathway, I can work on any feelings of guilt, inadequacy or self-blame my mind may trigger. I may even see how useless it is to buy into the right-wrong tapes my mind keeps running that can crystallize my anger into hatred—and keep me from loving myself or the other driver.

I can see all of this as an opportunity to become aware of my addictions (Third Pathway). We are all children of the universe. We set up the soap operas that give us the lessons we need. My car wreck was not an "accident." It's all part of learning to be "at home" on planet Earth.

BUYING IN

We use the phrase "buying in" as a shortcut way of saying "getting caught up emotionally in their predicaments." Let's look at how we can use the Eighth Pathway in a minute-to-minute way with the people around us. Most of the time when people with whom we interact are running addictions, we will unconsciously buy into their stuff and make the melodrama "real" in our minds. When we ignore the Eighth Pathway and buy into people's stuff, we keep ourselves trapped in the illusion that life is a big problem and they're in trouble. We help them validate the separate-self tapes they are running that keep them stuck in the mental patterns of resisting, clinging and ignoring.

We pass on the living spirit of love when we can listen to people with our hearts and minds equally, when we can love them no matter how "unconscious" their tapes, and when we simply put out a vibration of "you are beautiful, capable and lovable." It helps if we do not push our thoughts upon them even though they be wise ones, and do not buy in and commiserate with them.

Thus we see that when we do not buy into the predicament of others, but just play our parts in loving and serving the world, we can create a more enjoyable and unifying experience of life. We don't have to buy into the tapes that make us create the illusions of the separate-self. The game is to keep loving and serving, loving and serving, loving and serving—and doing the constant inner work of spotting addictive tapes, making it emotionally O.K. to have them, using the Pathways, increasingly handling our addictive demands, and eventually dropping them.

So it boils down to loving everyone unconditionally— even when we don't like the drama someone is currently running. We can build a loving bridge from our hearts into the hearts of everyone around us **even if they don't maintain their part of the bridge.**

It doesn't necessarily take two people to play the love game. It doesn't require another person who knows and follows the rules. The love game is not an exchange—or a barter. IT ONLY TAKES YOU TO PLAY IT.

SEDUCTIVE SITUATIONS

Notice that "buying in" means **reacting with emotion-backed addictions to what someone does or says.** We tend to buy into each other's stuff so quickly and automatically that it's happening before we realize it. (See examples on

115

BUYING INTO THE PREDICAMENTS OF LIFE

Situation	Tapes Involving Buying In	Alternative Tapes
You're in a drugstore to buy toothpaste. You hand the cashier a $100 bill. She snaps angrily that you're giving her a hard time.	"It's a big enough store to have change. You shouldn't get angry at customers like that."	"I can understand your being angry. I don't have anything smaller. Life is giving me a message that sometimes people will feel imposed on when I give them a $100 bill."
Your friend's wife has been negative toward sex for the last two months and he is creating feelings of anger, resentment, inadequacy and separateness.	"It's really wrong when she doesn't love you enough to enjoy sex with you. Maybe you ought to find a girlfriend or consider leaving her."	"When people don't handle their emotion-backed demands, their feelings of love can decrease. Sexual sharing is affected. The problem is not you, or her, or even sex. When addictive demands go up, love goes down."
Your sister's marriage has just ended in divorce and she is creating an experience of fear, insecurity, resentment, anger, inadequacy and jealousy.	"He's awful to do that to you. I feel sorry for you. You're having a really bad time."	"I'm glad I can be with you when you're creating all these uncomfortable feelings. I know you don't feel beautiful and lovable right now, but I want you to know that my heart is tuned-in to the beautiful being you are, rather than the soap opera character of divorced person that you are playing to the hilt right now."
Your friend's son has just died and your friend is feeling sad, guilty and confused.	"I know it's a terrible thing to bear. It's such a catastrophe. It shouldn't have happened."	"I know how you feel and my heart is with you. Let's look at what we do have and not what we don't have. What we have is the joyous times we all shared when he was here, and the love for your son that we can always share."

opposite page.) We can react through our Power Center with anger or annoyance and prepare to knock heads. Or we may hook in through our Security Center with fear or worry.

In the first incident on the page "Buying Into the Predicaments of Life," the example given for buying into the situation is a power reaction. We could also buy into this situation with a fear, insecurity or self-rejection tape such as, "Oh, you're right. I'm so dumb. I'm always doing stupid things like this. Why can't I be more thoughtful?"

Triggering embarrassment, shame or guilt is just as much a case of buying in as pushing your anger button. The important thing to note is that buying in is based on how you feel inside. **It may or may not be expressed outwardly**—depending on whether your addiction is at the acting-out, emoting-out or thinking-out strength.

You can learn to agree or disagree without buying in emotionally. You can still deal with a situation **by asking for what you want, and doing what you want**—and not buy in. You just don't respond to things by letting yourself get hooked into the illusions of the separate-self of either yourself or others. You see your drama and their drama from a mountaintop perspective—instead of through the stuffy tunnels of security, sensation or power.

STAYING CONSCIOUS

One way to use the Eighth Pathway is to put your own name or someone else's name into the Pathway. It might then say, "I feel with loving compassion the problems of Mary without getting caught up emotionally in her predicaments that are offering her messages she needs for her growth." Thus the Eighth Pathway can help you create a space between you and what's happening—so you won't take the soap opera so seriously. You can also use this Pathway as a door to the Conscious-awareness Center. This Center of Consciousness will be explained in Chapter 14.

117

As you begin to do your inner work, you can honor the lessons that life is offering you and other people. You will notice that in each of the four situations we have described, life is just offering a teaching which is being resisted, and not experienced as a richness—or at least as an opportunity to grow. It's so easy to see the teaching that **other people are resisting in their lives!**

But remember, **you can't force growth on other people.** It will not help to accuse them of not using the here-and-now situation in their lives for consciousness growth. The more you push people to get them to work on themselves, the more their egos and minds will create separateness from you—and also resist the growth process. Work on any addiction you may have that people use their opportunities to grow. We all grow when we're ready to grow—and not before. **The most you can do for others is to work on yourself. THIS IS PROFOUNDLY TRUE.**

So what do you do when your friend is creating alienation, separateness, misery, anxiety, worry, irritation, fear, anger, jealousy, boredom, guilt, hostility, disappointment, disgust, annoyance, revulsion, frustration, helplessness, hopelessness, impatience or other separating feelings? **When you find yourself buying into someone's stuff, you just repeat the Eighth Pathway silently for a few minutes.** Then say all of the Twelve Pathways several times to further increase your insight.

This inner work can help you be a creative cause in your life instead of an effect of the other person's melodrama. You may then feel like flowing energy into loving and serving them. But it won't be from pity, fear and worry. You'll just be playing your part in sharing your energy—and helping the world work better. You will enjoy your life more—and also create a vibrational space of sanity, love and genuine helpfulness. You will then intuitively know how you can more effectively love and serve a brother or sister. And more effectively loving and serving will some-

Eighth Pathway: I feel with loving compassion the problems of others without getting caught
up emotionally in their predicaments that are offering them
messages they need for their growth.

times take the form of doing nothing. Don't be addicted to cultural forms. Follow your intuitive feelings . . . .

You can thus see the Eighth Pathway as adding to your skill in helping you **"Love everyone unconditionally— including yourself."** It helps you go beyond a roller-coastering love that gets scrambled up in the soap opera of life. It helps you be with people without your confirming and deepening the illusions they are creating by resisting, clinging or ignoring.

The use of the Eighth Pathway helps in freeing you from buying into any folkways of our culture that increase your separateness, alienation, neurosis, sickness and unhappiness. When synchronized with the others, the Eighth Pathway will help you take another step toward getting in touch with the beautiful being that you really are—and with the beautiful being that lies within everyone else.

I act freely when I am tuned-in, centered and loving, but if possible I avoid acting when I am emotionally upset and depriving myself of the wisdom that flows from love and expanded consciousness.

12
easy does it

THE NINTH PATHWAY BEGINS with a beautiful affirmation of your basic intelligence—your basic goodness. It proclaims, "I act freely when I am tuned-in, centered and loving . . . ." "Tuned-in" means aware and mindful. It means that what your mind automatically selects for you to notice is not being distorted by your addictive demands. You're tuned-in to the environment around you. You're tuned-in to the vibrations of people around you. You're tuned-in to your body and your feelings. And you're tuned-in to your mind with its vast memory banks and its ingenious manipulative and logical capabilities.

"Centered" means that you are balanced and comfortable right where you are. You're not running toward something that you're addictively demanding, and you're not running away from something you're resisting. You're creating a here-and-now harmony with yourself and the world around you. And from this vantage point, you can comfortably deal with whatever needs doing.

"Loving" means that your mind is not maintaining brick walls (or even bamboo curtains!) between you and the people around you. You may not approve of everything they do and say in the melodrama of life, but you can compassionately understand where they're coming from. You see as cause and effect that their programming makes them do what they do.

When you are loving, the distinction between self and others loses its hard, bold line of difference. You know that they have a human heart just like yours—and **you** maintain a bridge of love connecting **your** heart with their heart. Loving means **you're** emotionally accepting. It means you're breaking through whatever makes **you** feel separate. It means that **you're** keeping them in **your** heart space.

POWER FROM THE LOVE CENTER

The Ninth Pathway thus tells you that you can "act freely" when these conditions are met: you are tuned-in, centered and loving. Does "acting freely" mean that you can use power in interpersonal situations without activating your separate-self? Yes! Some people may be surprised to learn that love and power may go together under certain conditions.

Of course, love and **separate-self** "me-vs.-you" power are not compatible. The more you have of one, the less you will have of the other. But power may be used by the unified-self for the mutual benefit of "me and you" or "us." For example, a mother may express her loving and caring by forcing her child to stop eating too many cookies. If she is tuned-in, centered and loving, she will be using **power from the Love Center of Consciousness for their mutual benefit.**

Separate-self power has usually been involved when you have used force: "You are invading my territory and I'm going to make you stop." You may have an addictive demand that someone who loves you not oppose you in anything. How often have you said, "If you really loved me you would . . . ."? But as we keep pointing out, what you love is the human being. You may or may not like the role someone is playing in that moment in the soap opera of life. And you're always free to play the antagonist role in his/her soap opera.

Now let's compare the use of power from the Power Center with power through the Love Center. Addictive "me-vs.-you" power is usually accompanied by separating feelings in both you and the person you're interacting with. You always run the risk that you or the other person will not fully work through this separateness and get clear at a later date. And week by week the separating feelings will feed upon themselves. Thus people who often use power to force their addictive demands can create enormous walls of separateness between themselves and other people.

Power from the Love Center is not ultimately separating. Suppose you are insisting that someone hurry up so you can see the beginning of a movie. If you can maintain a clear love space for this person while you are confronting him or her, s/he will most likely get angry—but s/he will also pick up your feeling of love. Although s/he may resist hurrying, the unconditional love you feel will help the person let go of the addictive demand—and not solidify any separating feelings. Behind the drama, the person you are confronting will tend to reflect your loving space. **You know that it will be all right. It's just passing stuff in today's soap opera.**

As you use the Pathways, you begin to realize that you get the most from your life when you **work on yourself to love people**—instead of running an interpersonal popularity contest to get people to love you. All you have to do is to open up your heart space. You can then act freely in the melodrama of life—and be really real. **You don't have to buy into people's stuff, you don't have to do everything they want you to do, you don't have to make yourself feel separate even when they say angry things to you, and you don't have to "give in" when you know it would be an unwise thing to do. YOU CAN LEARN TO SAY "NO" WITHOUT FEELING SEPARATE.**

Let's not power trip ourselves while we are learning not to power trip others. While we are learning to handle our power addictions, we can be loving and compassionate toward ourselves and accept ourselves even when we act from separate-self power. We can accept ourselves if we throw someone out of our hearts when we are demanding to get our way. We're not "bad" when we run addictive power. It's just not the most effective way to love ourselves and others. There is a higher level of skill than the subject-object jungle type of power. But let's make it O.K. to be where we are right now—and let's also benefit from the lessons that life is offering us for our consciousness growth.

DELAYED ACTIONS

The Ninth Pathway suggests that **you can trust yourself and act freely when you are in the Love Center.** But suppose you're not in the Love Center. What if your addictive demands are triggering fear, frustration or anger? In this situation, the Ninth Pathway recommends, ". . . if possible I avoid acting when I am emotionally upset . . . ." (The phrase "if possible" recognizes exceptions, as in the case of a physical emergency. If the house is on fire, forget about the Ninth Pathway. Go ahead and act fast even though you're emotionally upset.)

123

When you respond to someone aggressively and angrily, you set up an intense melodrama between yourself and another person. It's not serious (sometimes that's hard to remember!)—but it does have consequences. You not only have to handle your anger and feelings of alienation and separateness, but you're also going to have to deal with the angry response the other person will create—unless s/he is solidly in the Love Center and not buying into your stuff.

Something that started out as a simple situation (involving perhaps one addiction of yours) can expand into a busy soap opera in which both of you may have gotten in touch with a half-dozen addictions. If you are using the situation for consciousness growth, this opportunity to practice the Pathways represents a gift of the universe. It also keeps you in "hot water."

As we begin to handle our addictive demands, we may want to simplify things. We may find it more enjoyable to create less turmoil in our lives. The jungle-type "shock" that occurs to our nervous systems and bodies when our addictive demands are triggered may not help us produce the most skillful responses to the complex situations of our multifaceted social lives. That's when we begin to use the Ninth Pathway to introduce **a conscious delay** that will give us a chance to use the Pathways instead of automatically reacting with addictive programming.

As students of consciousness, we may wish to **provide a space between us and our life situations.** This lets us look consciously at our addictive demands, see the distortions they are introducing into our perceptions, and be aware of the separateness caused by our automatic, addictive action patterns. When we delay our actions, our basic inner wisdom has a chance to become operative as we repeat the Pathways to ourselves. The Ninth Pathway suggests that we give ourselves **a brief time** to do the inner work needed to escape from the blindness temporarily induced by our addictions.

When we have put a lot of angry energy into our environment, **even if we get free from the grip of our own addictions, we still may be surrounded by angry, upset people.** Taking the time to use the Pathways helps us avoid the up-and-down roller-coastering that we create when we energetically act out our addictive demands. As we get more skillful in using the Pathways, we can avoid "flying off the handle" and triggering addictions in other people that complicate our melodrama.

Although most of our discussion has dealt with delaying our addictive power responses to a situation, the Ninth Pathway is equally useful when we have security or sensation addictions. In the panic of security addictions or the "urgency" of sensation addictions, we may set up more problems for ourselves. A reasonable delay that gives us a chance to handle our addictions may help us improve our skills in getting the most from our lives.

THE DOUBLE BIND

The Ninth Pathway puts you in an interesting double bind with the Seventh Pathway. The Seventh tells you to open yourself genuinely to all people by communicating your deepest feelings. The Ninth advises you to avoid acting when you're emotionally upset. So what do you do if you've pushed your addiction button and are making yourself feel angry toward someone? Do you communicate that anger or do you hold up your angry words to give yourself a chance to work on your addiction?

Let's not misuse the "if possible I avoid acting" portion of the Ninth Pathway as an excuse to avoid working on ourselves—or for suppressing. A delay of ten minutes or an hour to do your inner work may be helpful. But if you were to avoid expressing your real feelings for an entire day, you may be losing this opportunity for growth. You may be creating a phony front that keeps you from genuinely enjoying love, peace and happiness in your life. So give yourself time to do the inner work. But sometimes you'll have to "blow the whistle" by telling your mind that it has had enough time to work on the addiction. Then use the Seventh Pathway to express your feelings and your addictive demands to the person involved.

In my experience, there are many addictive situations in which this delay suggested by the Ninth Pathway is helpful. And I have also known addictive demands that I was not able to handle in a reasonable time with my existing skill in doing the inner work. When I went back to the Seventh Pathway and opened myself genuinely to people, I found that the illusion of separateness often melted away—and I felt warm, close and loving again.

So be honest with yourself. If it isn't happening, be sure to use the Seventh Pathway, which says to ". . . open myself genuinely to all people by being willing to fully communicate my deepest feelings since hiding in any degree keeps me stuck in my illusion of separateness from other people."

THE WISDOM THAT FLOWS FROM LOVE

The Ninth Pathway also tells us why we may act more appropriately if we briefly delay our actions in order to work on an addictive demand. It points out that when we are emotionally upset, we are depriving ourselves "of the wisdom that flows from love and expanded consciousness." Unconditional love that is not addictively demanding anything brings a wisdom to our thoughts and actions. As we've noted, wisdom is not found in the scalpel-like discriminations of the rational mind. Nor is it found in the sentimental, indulgent feelings of the heart.

Wisdom is always a blend of head and heart. As you up-level addictions to preferences, you will more fully love yourself and others. From the love space, you'll know what you need to do **to perfectly integrate "what is" in your life with your needs and desires.** That will be the form that wisdom has for you at this here-and-now situation in your life.

You'll know that you know—and it will be a feeling of "that's it" which needs no proof. If this isn't happening, perhaps your addictive demands have blocked your wise integration of all of the factors. You may put too much emphasis on rejecting some things (resisting), hanging on to some things (clinging), or overlooking others (ignoring). Addictive demands unbalance the mind and create thoughts and actions that keep us stumbling and bumbling through life.

The Ninth Pathway gives you a strong clue for operating your biocomputer in a way that enables you to tune-in to the wisdom that lies within you. It tells you that wisdom flows from (1) love and (2) expanded consciousness. Your mind is incredibly wise. But your wisdom is blocked.

It's like we have a pot of gold—but can't get at it. It's as though we have a bright light, but it is thoroughly boxed in by our addictive demands, and this keeps us living in a dim shadow world. We're so busy acting out, emoting out and thinking out our security, sensation and power addictions that the screen of our consciousness has no space for the subtler nuances of our basic wisdom and intuitive clarity. Our thoughts and actions are so separating that they do not help us get the most that's gettable in our lives. We lack the fine-line tuning that enables us to find the wise place between too little and too much.

FACTORS OF EXPANDED CONSCIOUSNESS

The words "expanded consciousness" in the Ninth Pathway do not refer to some exalted, far-out trance-like state of mind. Instead, "expanded consciousness" simply means that we are not resisting, clinging to or ignoring things which need to be taken into consideration and integrated into our thoughts and actions. Expanded consciousness as Joseph Goldstein points out may be viewed as **a balancing of seven mental factors:**

1. **Mindfulness:** Broad awareness of "what is" instead of ignoring or not noticing important aspects of the here and now.

2. **Wisdom:** Balancing all of the factors of the head and the heart so as to produce a skillful and compassionate response to life instead of a confused, inappropriate response due to overemphasizing some factors and underemphasizing others. Wisdom is seeing the overall picture.

3. **Energy:** An energetic participation in the games of life instead of a lazy, sluggish approach.

4. **Rapture:** An interest or fascination with life instead of a bored, dulled, grayed-out feeling.

5. **Tranquillity:** A calmness, serenity and inner peace instead of a frantic, threatened, overly emotional handling of the here and now.

6. **Concentration:** An ability to focus the mind on what's now instead of a butterfly-like flitting around that doesn't come to grips with a situation long enough to find a skillful response.

7. **Equanimity:** An equal-valued perception of the games of life as not personally threatening, as opposed to experiencing things as heavy in their consequences with doom always around the corner.

When these seven factors are operating **simultaneously,** the mind has an "expanded consciousness." This means that the mind is functioning at its highest potential. When all seven factors are balanced, you can create a maximum experience of enjoyment and at the same time do the most appropriate thing interacting with the world around you.

Bit by bit, you're tooling up to meet the greatest challenge that life could offer you—the job of extricating you from you. It's rescuing the beautiful essential you from the separating mental habits that you happened to pick up in the past. It's helping you see beyond who you think you are so that who you really are can be actualized. It's a remodeling job on your programming.

You're going beyond an edifice of personality that is as good as most—but not really skillful enough to create a loving, happy life. You are beginning a reconstruction of your motivational systems that have in the past been almost solely preoccupied with the separate-self demands of more security, more sensation and more power—which turns out to be a bottomless pit.

Our explorations into the unified-self are opening up the possibility of transforming our lives. We go from inner poverty to riches as we acquire skill in turning down our addictive demands and turning up our love. We begin to see that this is not only the fulfillment of our individual lives, but it is the only way that we can go beyond our strident political, social and economic conflicts to create a world of cooperativeness, harmony and love. We're not only rescuing ourselves—we're doing our part in saving the world, too!

PART V

Discovering My Conscious-Awareness

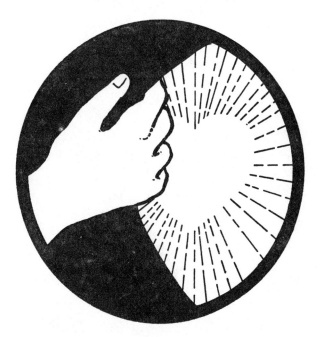

I am continually calming the restless scanning of my rational mind in order to perceive the finer energies that enable me to unitively merge with everything around me.

13

quieting the mind

Lᴵᴷᴱ ꜰᴵʀᴱ, ᴛʜᴱ ʀᴀᴛᴵᴏɴᴀʟ ᴍᴵɴᴅ is a great servant—but a terrible master. The purpose of all of the Twelve Pathways is to help us become the masters of our minds so that we can create the finest possible experience of our lives. And mastery of the mind requires a mastery of our addictive demands, which can distort what we feel, think, say and do.

Just as our other senses are our "friends" that help us orient ourselves, our logical-intellectual-rational functions are likewise designed to be our "friends." The mind juggles our incoming sensory data, selected items in our memory banks and our desire systems so that, hopefully, we can use what's here and now to get what we want from life. But as said before, except in the discipline of science, when it surrenders to the impartial measurements of the laboratory, our rational minds are not really concerned with selfless "truth." The intellect focuses on helping us deal with the here and now in the light of our core beliefs (which may be erroneous) and our addictive demands (which are often impractical). (See "core belief" in glossary.) It turns out an endless stream of thoughts, giving us good-sounding reasons for everything we feel, think, say and do. Our minds often win the game of being right and lose the game of heart-to-heart loving.

LOVE GAME VS. RIGHT-WRONG GAME

The more that you are actually "right" (and another person actually "wrong"), the more likely that you are creating and living in a subjective reality that limits your overall insight and traps you in a "me-vs.-them" jungle consciousness. Unless your rational mind follows up on the subtle cues from your "heart" or intuitive wisdom, **it has great difficulty in discovering that it is "off base"** and creating unnecessary separateness, noncooperativeness and turmoil. It will not see that it is making a life situation unnecessarily difficult or unworkable. **When you're "rightest," you may do the "wrongest" things—which lead you to alienate yourself.**

On the other hand, whenever you are "wrong," your rational mind will most likely have the strongest and most persuasive defenses, "on tap" for instant use. Thus when you're "wrongest," you'll probably feel "rightest." And if you're surrounded by people who agree you're right (your "true friends," of course), you're almost certain to crystallize into an addictive, separating consciousness with someone you think is "wrong." As Carole Lentz, Director of

Cornucopia, puts it, "When you're running an addiction and a friend buys into your separating addictive feelings— one plus one equals truth!"

The next time you feel hard-nosed right, try seeing the penalties you are paying for snowballing all that separateness. Love is more important than forcing someone to agree you're right. The love connection between your heart and the hearts of those around you can help your life work a hundred times better than "being right." **Nothing is more important than the love space.** Making yourself "right" and the other person "wrong" may be O.K. in the give-and-take of life—but don't let it turn off your heart space with the person. The right-wrong game can keep you trapped in the separate-self.

When you love someone even if s/he is wrong (and perhaps trying to make you look wrong), you can still ask for what you want. You can go ahead and do what you want to do. You can even yell or pound the desk. You don't have to have their approval or validation. **But never throw a human being out of your heart.** Keep that heart connection behind the soap opera that both of you are acting out. **Do it even if the other person doesn't.**

Work on your addictive demand that people be fair, reasonable, admit you're right or meet you halfway. You'll enjoy your life more from the cool elevation of the unified-self. Your life will become a series of enjoyable games instead of a series of heavy problems. And people will have a better chance of working through their addictions if you keep loving them in your heart. A good test of your skill in loving unconditionally is to be able to throw someone out of your house, but not throw them out of your heart even for a moment!

Look at how things have happened in your life with your wife, husband, children, parents, lovers, friends and business associates. Based on your own life experiences, how many of the following can you validate?

135

Love is more important than your precious image. Love is more important than money. Love is more important than rules. Love is more important than being right. Love is more important than efficiency. Love is more important than sleep. Love is more important than sex. Love is more important than being on time. Love is more important than getting your own way. Love is more important than doing what you want to do. Love is more important than the taste of food. Love is more important than people meeting your models. Love is more important than your plans. Love is more important than having time alone. Love is more important than your success. Love is more important than your health. Love is more important than your pride or prestige. Love is more important than a skinny figure. LOVE IS MORE IMPORTANT THAN ANYTHING ELSE!

When you make love more important than anything else in your life, you actually set up your life to increase the chances of getting the other things. You can still put out energy to get what you want. Your unflickering love throughout the daily give-and-take of life will be reflected back to you in the form of increased helpfulness and cooperation—and love and caring. People begin to deeply trust you when they know **that you know** that you'd lose more than you'd gain if you get what you want—but neglect to do the inner work when needed to love yourself and others.

When you clearly know that love helps your life work better than anything else, you will be ready for an accelerated rate of growth. From then on, your inner work will be to straighten out the emotion-backed, addictive programs and core beliefs that automatically put you in conflict with your new understanding of how basically important it is to **"Love everyone unconditionally—including yourself"** even when (or especially when) someone isn't meeting your models. You'll develop an ability to let go that lets you tell yourself, "I'll take what life may give me when I'm loving more and demanding less. It's enough. I can see the heavy price I pay in blocking love and cooperation. I don't have to demand more than people can **naturally** give me when they love me—and perceive me as 'us.'"

And once you do this inner work, your life will most likely give you—without efforting—more than you could possibly need of what you thought you "gave up." We live in a cornucopia. Life is set up to work. And yet we've been turning it off by the way we've been demanding more and loving less.

THE RESTLESS SCANNING

The Tenth Pathway begins, "I am continually calming the restless scanning of my rational mind." Have you noticed the way your mind incessantly comes up with thought after thought after thought? In psychoanalysis, this is called "free association." The mind is "never" still when you're awake. Even in sleep it may be active in producing the free-form expressions of your addictive demands known as dreams. Your mind never quiets itself unless you are in deep sleep. It's just one endless thought after another. The Tenth Pathway calls this "the restless scanning of my rational mind."

When you are aware that the world is not fitting one of your addictive models, the restless scanning of the rational mind becomes like water when it is bouncing around in the rapids. It is turbulent, tricky, fast—and dangerous from the point of view of making life work well. As the water goes beyond the rapids into the wide, smooth part of the river, it is still moving—but not turbulently so. By analogy, this would represent the mind in its handling of preferences. It is still restlessly scanning, but it is slowed down to a mellower pace—and it is no longer dangerous from the point of view of balanced perception.

Continuing this analogy, when the water reaches the calm lake, it moves even more slowly and it can be almost still. By analogy, one's mind is no longer driven by addictions or even high-level preferences. One may then begin to notice a few seconds in which the mind may stop its continuous production of thoughts. The senses still report sight and sounds. And one has the beautiful experience of just being tuned-in to both inside and outside one's body without the tension of desire or the rapid flow of words that affect one's inner peace.

In ordinary life, one's mind will be active enough to continue producing thoughts. We would not want to set up a goal of going minute after minute in the middle of one's life activities without a flow of thoughts. This would not be at all realistic. But it is possible, as one uplevels addictions to preferences, to become more aware of wordless gaps in the output of the rational mind. It is possible to be able to briefly turn off the stream of internal words for a few seconds at will. This silent awareness of tuning-in to "what's now" without the distractions of words and more words is a sign of the beginning of mastery of one's rational mind activity.

In many consciousness paths, meditation is used in calming the restless scanning of the rational mind. In the Living Love Way, we use "meditation in action." In the hurly-burly of daily life, we work on **handling our addictions** or upleveling them to preferences. It is our addictive demands that make the mind resist, cling and ignore, and thus produce turmoil. As we continue to "welcome the opportunity" to work on ourselves in the here-and-now situations in our lives, we can gradually learn to **prefer** that the melodrama of our lives go a certain way—but behind all that, we realize that it's all melodrama and it really doesn't matter. From a panoramic perspective of our life as a whole, we can see it all with equanimity. As we uplevel addictions to preferences, our minds begin to calm down—and we increasingly experience inner peace and serenity.

THE FINER ENERGIES

The Tenth Pathway tells you that when you calm the restless scanning of your rational mind, you can perceive the finer (or more subtle) energies. This does not refer to metaphysical planes of existence beyond ordinary life. When you're running an addiction, your mind is restlessly scanning at a rapid pace. It tells itself there is much to be lost or gained. What the Tenth Pathway is saying is simply that when you perceive the world through preferential programming, your mind will calm down. Its activity becomes more like the wavelets gently lapping against the side of a canoe rather than storm waves that jostle the canoe about and threaten to overturn it.

To see how tuned-in you are to the finer energies around you, close your eyes right now and describe to yourself what's in the room around you. Sometime when you are with several people, close your eyes and describe the psychological space that each one of them is in. Have you really been looking into their eyes, noticing their body language, and hearing what they are communicating beyond their words? **Or are you so concentrated on your own thoughts and desires that you've hardly noticed other people at all?**

You don't have to be a psychic or gifted with extrasensory perception to tune-in to the finer energies in the environment. You simply create large enough gaps between your addictions so that you are free of the "storms." **It means fully opening the doors of your perception to be aware of what the world is constantly telling you about itself. It boils down to just noticing.**

UNITIVELY MERGING

The Tenth Pathway ends by explaining the benefit of perceiving the finer energies: to "unitively merge with everything around me." "Unitively merging" is not to be taken in a literal, physical sense. The molecules of your body will not merge with the molecules of someone else's body or with the trees, automobiles or sofas. The unitive merging implies a non-definiteness of the boundaries of what is "me" and what is "not me." This merging experience means that you create an empathetic, intuitive feeling that everything "outside your skin" is just another part of you. The "me-vs.-you" experience diminishes. As the addictions that create the illusory experience of the separate-self dominate the mind less and less, this unitive experience has an opportunity to expand.

As you rely upon this intuitive (as opposed to rational, cerebral or intellectual) knowing, your remarkable mind can increase its awareness of that which is both inside and outside your skin. And when your ego is not running off separate-self tapes, the boundary of your own skin becomes less important, and your experience of your unified-self can be enlarged enormously. It is only when people or situations are perceived as nonthreatening that you can experience them in a unitive mode.

LET IT HAPPEN

I wish to emphasize time and time again that all of the things described in this chapter (as well as the other chapters of this book) automatically happen when you consistently work on yourself **to uplevel your addictions to preferences.** If you try to force your mind to become calm, or to perceive the finer energies, or to unitively merge, it will not work as well. It will all happen as a natural operation of your wonderful mind as you turn down your addictions and turn up your love.

It is helpful to have a map that enables you to know where you are and what you may next expect to see down the road. Similarly, you can just be aware of the things that are described in this chapter, relate them to what is actually happening in your mind, and be particularly tuned-in to any brief moments when (1) the restless scanning of your mind momentarily stops, (2) your perception of finer energies is increased and (3) a flash of unitively merging is experienced.

At first it may be for only a few seconds at a time. If you don't notice these moments, your growth will be slowed. If you tune-in to these brief experiences, you will be consciously reinforcing these functional patterns of mind activity so that they may become increasingly more available in the future.

Always remember that consciousness growth is just a game you are playing with yourself—and the world. It is not who you really are—for behind all of the activities of the mind and body, and your melodramatic games of interacting with the environment and people around you, there lies your essence—your Conscious-awareness—**that part of you which is aware that it is aware.** Your essence is that part of you which is nonjudgmentally aware of the printout that the ego and mind choose for the screen of your consciousness. It is that part of you beyond self-consciousness that is not good or bad, right or wrong, fair or unfair, true or false or any of the opposites—it just silently is.

I am constantly aware of which of the Seven Centers of Consciousness I am using, and I feel my energy, perceptiveness, love and inner peace growing as I open all of the Centers of Consciousness.

14

turning on your wisdom

IN THE LIVING LOVE WAY, WE formulate seven Centers of Consciousness. These are effective tools for increasing our insight into the desire systems that are determining our thoughts and are thus controlling our actions moment by moment. These Centers act as filters that process our incoming sensory data, selection of memories, and flow of thoughts, from the point of view of a preselected goal.

As we've frequently mentioned, the Security, Sensation and Power Centers of Consciousness were perfected for survival in the jungle, and have been used by our ancestors for millions of years. Although we are now seldom in danger of being eaten by an animal, our minds tend to create threatening survival situations out of the ordinary back and forth of our daily lives. By automatically using these first three Centers, we unconsciously create the jungle mentality of the separate-self.

The Security, Sensation and Power Centers of Consciousness keep us trapped in the illusion that life is a "me-vs.-them" battle. Incoming sensory data and information from our memory banks are all twisted into a conceptual split between self and others. This makes the separate-self seem solid and real! **Since the separate-self programming is self-confirming, we trap ourselves in the illusion that this separateness is the way life is—instead of being aware that it is created by the mechanisms of our minds.**

Here are the Seven Centers of Consciousness that will be explained in this chapter:

1. **The Security Center** ⎫
2. **The Sensation Center** ⎬ SEPARATE-SELF
3. **The Power Center** ⎭

4. **The Love Center** ⎫
5. **The Cornucopia Center** ⎪ UNIFIED-
6. **The Conscious-Awareness Center** ⎬ SELF
7. **The Cosmic Consciousness Center** ⎭

THE SECURITY CENTER

Let's look at the first of the jungle centers—the Security Center. The dominating emotion triggered when things do not meet our security addictions is fear. Other allied emotions that may be created by security addictions are worry, anxiety, guilt, nervousness, horror, terror, disappointment, hurt, panic, confusion, sadness, embarrassment, shame, grief, apprehension, loneliness, helplessness, de-

143

spair, doubt, pity and jealousy. When our addictions trigger these emotions, we create the deepest illusions of separateness and alienation. We are trapped in a subject-object way of experiencing and relating to the people around us. They become objects to manipulate in order to increase our security. The only people that are important when we are running security addictions are the people who threaten us and the people who can help us. Everybody else tends to be ignored as unimportant.

Living in fear, worry and anxiety represents the bottom of the barrel in terms of human enjoyment. Continued anxiety and worry psychosomatically tear our bodies apart by creating illnesses and nervous breakdowns. Although the Security Center can direct great bursts of energy (as when running from a tiger), in the long run it blocks the natural flow of energy. When we run security tapes, our aliveness is at a minimum—in fact, we can hardly speak of aliveness. Our experience is better described in terms of misery, unhappiness and "what's the use of it all?" We thus see that running security tapes produces low energy and little real involvement with people—we join the "living dead." When we're worried, we may sleep twelve hours a day and still be tired.

There is a wisdom in our minds providing us with low energy when we feel insecure. When we are running security tapes, we have the least clarity and perceptiveness. Were we to be energetic at these times, we might act out so many separating illusions that we would enormously complicate our melodramas. How wise it is that our minds provide us with the lowest levels of energy when our illusions are the greatest!

CREATING SECURITY

There are real dangers to life and limb in our environment, and we need to be responsive to these. If we don't run security tapes, wouldn't we be likely to walk in front of a car and get killed? How do we create security in life without the fears triggered by addictive security tapes? Aren't we really more careful when we're afraid? It is crucial to understand clearly the answers to these reasonable questions to give our minds a solid basis for working on our security addictions.

Our animal ancestors (who successfully transmitted our genes from generation to generation for millions of years) did not have the remarkable human cortex to work with. Their minds were incapable of the cause-effect understandings that we can quickly "flash on" and use for our safe guidance. If we had the mental equipment that our ancestors had fifty million years ago, we too would need to use the Security Center to create the experience of fear which would make us trembly-cautious or perhaps run away from the situation entirely.

Let's examine how awareness is more protective than addictive fear. Suppose you want to cross a busy thoroughfare with four lanes of traffic speeding back and forth. This could kill you just as quickly as any lion in the jungle. But to the extent that your nervous system triggers fear (with a pounding heart and that emotional gripping and urgency that you feel when you are afraid), **you will be less safe when crossing the street.** As a human being, your best mechanism for survival in this street-crossing situation lies not in your activation of the fearful security tapes. Instead, you just stand on the sidewalk and use your mind to calmly increase your **awareness** of the flow of the traffic in front of you. You'll notice that cars tend to come in bunches, and you can be totally relaxed while you wait for the gaps to occur simultaneously in the various lanes of traffic. When you see a sufficient gap about to happen, you can ready yourself to cross the street. As this opening unfolds, with a pace slightly above normal, you can cross the street in complete safety without the slightest feeling

145

of fear. **Thus, by being alert to your environment and by using insights based on your experience,** you can go beyond the need for addictive security programming. Let's take another type of example. Suppose halfway through a jet flight, the outside engine on the right wing catches fire. Would you want a pilot who would strongly activate his or her Security Center of Consciousness? Would you want his or her heart to race madly with adrenalin pumping rapidly through the bloodstream? Would you be safer if the pilot's consciousness were dominated by fear? Would a pilot who is really scared be able to make the intricate, rapid responses needed to give maximum control over the situation?

Or would you prefer to have a pilot who would notice that the jet engine was on fire, and immediately in one, two, three fashion begin the fire control procedures known to be most effective in this emergency? Wouldn't you rather have a pilot who without trembling could tell the engineer to shut off fuel to the engine and to activate the fire extinguishing equipment with a clear overall awareness of the situation? Wouldn't you want a fearless pilot who, without screaming, could tell the radio operator to notify the nearest airport of what was happening and your impending arrival—and who would then get on the PA system and share with the passengers in a calm and realistic manner exactly what was happening and what was being done?

In other words, even in these situations where life may actually be in danger, the jungle security programming with its trembling and fear seems least likely to offer an adult human being the greatest possible security. Yet Security Center programming constantly **gives you the illusion that fear is an appropriate response to many of our life situations.** The skillful use of the Pathways can help you to go beyond these limitations of the Security Center of Consciousness.

THE SENSATION CENTER

Our addictive programming may make us act compulsively when food or sex opportunities are available. But such automatic, compulsive reacting to these delightful sensory possibilities destroys an overall balance that can result in less total enjoyment than we would otherwise have. Addictive desires in both food and sex (or any other sensation) can constantly keep us creating separateness with ourselves and others. From the point of view of the unified-self, food and sex are there for our wise use and enjoyment. It's our addictive demands that make us pushy, over-hungry and greedy. Our addictions make us create the experience of deficiency—when we actually have enough to be happy. They block our enjoyment of life. They make us clumsy, rather than skillful, to the degree that we act out, emote out and think out our addictive resisting, clinging or ignoring.

In this description of the Sensation Center of Consciousness, we will talk about food and sex, but the same considerations apply equally to other sensations that we addictively run after—or avoid. These other sensation addictions can include such things as music, sunsets, hot or cold climate, a soft or hard bed, pain in our bodies, an addiction to feeling high such as may occur with drugs, and so forth. When we're motivated by sensations, our experience of life, even when addictive, may not be as heavy as with the Security Center. However, we still lay ourselves open to such separating feelings as frustration, disappointment, boredom, disgust, jealousy, anguish and grief.

In general, we will have a greater flow of energy when our consciousness is sensation-dominated instead of security-dominated. We may tell ourselves that we are tired. But if an interesting opportunity for food or sex arises, our tiredness often has a magical way of disappearing! Sensation consciousness also brings us in contact with more people. Although it's still subject-object to a large extent, the Sensation Center offers us a lot more enjoyment of life than we'll ever find in the Security Center.

When our sensation addictions are being satisfied, our experiences can be enjoyable. Unfortunately, we may not be enjoying them for long. For when we try to create happiness through sensations, **they become less and less satisfying when unvaried and repeated in too short a period of time.** The nature of our nervous systems is that we can eventually bore ourselves with any sensation—however delightful. Thus, because of the way our minds create jadedness, dullness, satiety and boredom, sensations are not dependable **as a foundation** for happiness in life. Sensations can add to our enjoyment of the melodrama of life, **but something more stable must be used if we humans are to continuously enjoy our lives.**

As with the Security Center, we take a giant step forward in our consciousness growth when we realize that the game is to handle (or uplevel to preferences) the addictive sensation demands that our minds are required to slavishly live out. But notice: we do not need to remove food or sex from our lives. The game is to get rid of the addiction—not food or sex.

For example, sex as a preference may add to our enjoyment of life. Sex as an addiction is a booby trap. Instead of letting things happen, we try to force things to happen. We treat people as objects—as "him" or "her"—not "us." Addictions complicate our ability to wisely tune in to this delightful aspect of the soap opera of our lives. We forget that the world is set up to provide us with sex. It's usually our addictive demands that turn it off. The problem lies not in the sexual activity. It lies in our addictive motivational space that leaves us constantly vulnerable to frustration, alienation and separateness. It makes us treat people in separating ways.

THE POWER CENTER

Since the food supply in the jungle is limited, only a limited number of animals can live in a square mile of jungle. Each animal tends to protect against invaders the territory that it needs to have enough food. For a monkey, this will be a smaller area than for a lion. But whatever the size, most animals develop territorial boundaries that they maintain by power techniques.

In our civilized lives, we similarly develop strong feelings of "mine" and "not mine." Our territorial consciousness (usually interacting with our security consciousness) can even claim another human being as part of our territory: "This is my mate and you stay away or it's war between you and me." The separating emotions that are automatically triggered by the Power Center are anger, resentment, annoyance, irritation, hatred, frustration, rage, hostility, fury, disgust, indignation, impatience, jealousy, disdain and so forth.

You can simultaneously use any of the three separating Centers of Consciousness. For example, if someone steals your credit card, you may create the experience of anger through the Power Center and fear through the Security Center. If your lover pays attention to someone else, you may instantly turn on your Security, Sensation and Power Centers—and trigger a triple torrent of jealousy!

As with security and sensation consciousness, the Power Center continues to keep us trapped in the illusion of the separate-self. Life is seen as "a battle between me and the rest of the world. Everybody is trying to invade my territory and I have to continually fight them off." When the mind unconsciously impresses this "me-vs.-them" frame of reference upon our memory selection, incoming sensory data and thought production, we often create this illusion of separateness as a self-fulfilling prophecy. When we fight people to protect "our territory," they usually fight back.

149

This proves we were right to begin with—life really is a battle for survival. In this way we make our illusions seem "real."

It's interesting to note that most of the separating emotions connected with our various addictive programmings are unpleasant from start to finish. However, the primary emotion connected with the Power Center is anger, and this may be pleasant when we first trigger it. It can be temporarily enjoyed if it is "righteous anger." Eventually the adrenalin gets "stale" in our bloodstreams, for we have not used it for its original biological purpose of physical fight or flight. If we have a nervous system that continually keeps us caught up in the Third Center, we will be vulnerable to developing such psychosomatic ailments as ulcers, high blood pressure, migraine headaches and nervous tension.

The purpose of power is to make us secure and to give us peace of mind—but unfortunately it boomerangs when used addictively. No millionaire has enough money to stay out of the grip of his or her addictions that generate unhappy experiences. A person can have a brain full of knowledge (even two Ph.D. degrees) but s/he will still be vulnerable to unpleasant addictive programmings. A person can have powerful social roles, such as being a top movie star or the president of a multinational corporation, and still be miserable with anger, frustration or anxiety.

We're beginning to understand that the experience of "enoughness" cannot be maintained when we are primarily motivated by security, sensation and power addictions. Please keep reminding yourself that we're not talking about what we actually do in the soap opera. We're talking about our inner motivations, which determine our experiences of ourselves and the world around us. To enjoy our lives as much as possible, we must make the quantum leap into the Love Center.

THE LOVE CENTER

As we've pointed out, the Security, Sensation and Power Centers have a long history of operation over millions of years. "What is" in the world feeds through these Centers, which direct our thoughts and actions in certain set ways. Because addictive energy has been created by us for so many millions of years, we tend to regard it as appropriate and natural—it is usually mistaken for "human nature." To go beyond it so that we can live together in more satisfying ways requires inner work on ourselves.

Security, sensation and power addictions constantly create the separate-self of the jungle. As we learn to uplevel more and more addictions to preferences, as we learn to love everyone unconditionally—including ourselves (or especially ourselves!), and as we take more and more responsibility for what we create in our lives, **we begin to open the possibility of escaping from the automatic grip of this jungle programming of the mind.** As we do the inner work on ourselves using the Twelve Pathways, we can increasingly flow our energy through the Love Center of Consciousness.

THE LEAP FROM THE JUNGLE

When using our jungle consciousness it is normal to skip back and forth moment by moment from security to power to sensation to power to security to sensation, etc. Even though we are predominantly running a jungle consciousness, we will occasionally have a glimpse into the Love Center. But this is only a tantalizing taste. For we are still vulnerable to the addictive mental habits that are used when something does not fit our addictive models of how it should be. To be able to live in the Love Center in a variety of life situations, a lot of determined and skillful inner work is necessary. The Pathways can be used as precise tools to help us gradually do this inner work.

As you go from the self-consciousness of security to sensation, or from sensation to power, **your energy, real involvement with people, and enjoyment of life increase to some degree.** But the greatest increases come as you move from the three addictive Centers to the Love Center. In the Love Center, your energy is not constantly frittered away in running addictively toward or away from things. Although you may be very active physically, in your heart there is a deep inner peace—an inner stillness in the midst of activity. Since you do not waste your energy in bodily tension or in worrying, it feels as though your deep reservoirs of energy are never exhausted.

Your interaction with people undergoes a dynamic change as you move from jungle consciousness to the first stage of the unified-self—which we call the Love Center. Here the hard line of separateness between self and others is slowly dissolving. Since your energy and thought processes are no longer tied up trying to fill the bottomless pit of security, sensation and power addictions, you experience a surplus of energy that now flows outward into the world toward other people and into the environment.

You find that you experience such a richness that you are able to give away more and more of your energy, love, time, helpfulness, cooperativeness and material things without expecting, needing or wanting a return. You begin to feel like a conduit that is here to channel a part of life's energy to where it is most needed. When freed from the catacombs of the selfish, deficiency-ridden separate-self, your enthusiasm and energy can flow into the fun game of loving and serving the world in your own way.

This is quite a novelty for the ego-mind. Previously it had always given something away within a mental bookkeeping system that would enable you to get something back of equal or greater value—either now or in the future.

As you become free from your petty security, sensation and power demands on the world and on yourself, you experience a surplus of energy **that lets you engage in the satisfying activity of giving it away.** Instead of your involvement with people being cast in a subject-object, predatory, barter style, you become openhearted and openhanded, and are able to give without a consciousness of "giver and receiver." This is a genuine involvement with people cooperatively working back and forth so that all of our lives work better. And it also helps us take better care of the only planet we have!

Do not read the above paragraphs and decide that you **should** be more generous and loving. It is not helpful to look down the road at future milestones of growth and then try to push yourself into being there now. Don't give gifts you can't now emotionally afford to give. And don't reject yourself because you do not meet your mental standards of loving—for this would be an addiction.

Remember that you don't have to force yourself to be anything we're talking about in this book. You do not experience the Love Center when you push yourself or are judgmental of yourself. It will all happen in its own perfectly unfolding way as you use the Pathways to handle your addictions and eventually uplevel them to preferences. As this growth happens, you will naturally release the love that you are now keeping locked up in your heart.

LOVE HAS NO FORM

Love is a heart space. Love is not a helpful action, although your love may lead you to help people in many ways. Don't let your ego use love for power purposes, such as "If you really loved me you would . . . ." Since love has no form, this might or might not be so. Look into your heart feelings to determine whether **you** are loving. Handle any addictive demand that makes **you** feel separate.

As you grow in consciousness, you will flow your energy into loving and serving. Here again, do not be misled by form. **Love is the feeling of an open heart. It is a motivational energy.** You can't prove your love by your actions. **Love just is.**

If your activities aren't necessarily changed as you begin to live in the Love Center, what is changed? Let's say you are in the business of selling fruits and vegetables. You may be primarily motivated to do this from the Security Center. You may tell yourself you are just working for money so you can pay your bills. Or you may tell yourself that you are working for money so you can enjoy delightful sensations such as a good stereo system, a heated king-sized waterbed, gourmet food, or candlelit dinners with a sexually attractive companion. You would thus be motivated by the Sensation Center. Or suppose you view your work as a way to feel the prestige of having the biggest and best fresh produce market in town. If this were your predominant motivation, we would consider that you were coming from the Power Center of Consciousness that is concerned with pride, money, power and worldly success.

If your main motivation were to operate a fruit and vegetable market to offer nutritious food at the lowest possible prices to your brothers and sisters in the community, you would be operating your business from the Love Center. What you're doing may still add security, sensation and power to your life—you may enjoy being able to pay your bills, buy things you like, and be well thought of. But these would be fringe benefits that automatically come to you when your main flow of energy is into loving and serving.

From the Love Center, most (but not all) of your daily activities will be quite similar to things you would do and say from the other Centers. You'd still pay your electric bills, sweep the floor, try to satisfy your customers and put in many hours of work each day. The main difference created by the various Centers of Consciousness lies in your internal experience and the satisfaction that you feel. As a motivating principle, loving and serving can enable you to create a much happier life than a self-centered pursuit of **your** security, **your** sensation and **your** power (including **your** prestige, **your** pride and **your** worldly success).

Thus when your energy flows through the Love Center, you don't necessarily have to change jobs—unless you're in a job that rips people off. **You just change your primary motivation to that of loving and serving. This can greatly increase your satisfaction and enjoyment of your work.** And you won't even need an increase in salary—but you may well get one!

BENEFITS OF THE LOVE CENTER

From the Love Center, the possibility is now opened for continuously (or nearly continuously) enjoying your life. When your main direction of energy flows into loving and serving others, you increasingly experience your life as a nonaddictive love drama. For it is always up to you whether you love someone unconditionally or not. You are learning that as you grow into a love consciousness, the behavior of other people can become irrelevant to your love experience. You can always love someone even though you don't approve of his/her acts. **You don't need permission to love.** You just do it. You can even make it O.K. to not be involved with someone. You don't need involvement to love. **But you're hurting yourself if you destroy your own feeling of love toward any person on earth.** (This would be a good time to review the seven rip-offs in the section entitled "The Misery We Create" in Chapter 4.)

Regardless of whether people are able to accept your love and return it, **you can always give your love to them.** Your love programming is increasingly helping **you** to break through the boundaries of the separate-self to love people **no matter what they say or do.** To do this, you must avoid

155

letting yourself become addicted to people appreciating—or even receiving your gift of love. **When, as and if they are ready, they will open themselves to your love—as a part of their growth.** At last you're beginning to get control of the factors involved in living a joyous and happy life. The rule of "win some and lose some" (which the separate-self plays by) becomes less and less applicable beginning at the Love Center. You experience "winning" more and more continuously—**for just loving creates the experience of winning the game of life.**

For example, even though you "lose" a game of checkers, at the same time you can always "win" a game that's really worth playing—**the game of enjoying it all.** When checkers is not experienced through security or power filters, you can **LOVE IT ALL.** The separate-self wants to enhance its domain by winning the game; the unified-self uses checkers as a fun way to be with another person—and this enjoyment is not dependent on jumping the other person's king! You can relax. You are experiencing that you don't have to fight the world every inch of the way.

THE CORNUCOPIA CENTER

When you create your experience of life through the Cornucopia Center, you feel that your life is overflowing with **more than you need to be happy.** It's there without your effort. Abundance flows without your doing anything except loving more and demanding less! You're rich and getting richer with everything really worth having: energy, perceptiveness, insight, wisdom, love, joy, happiness and purpose! And no tax collector or catastrophe can threaten your true wealth—for it is securely inside you beyond the fluctuations of the soap opera.

My experience is that the Cornucopia Center of Consciousness simply begins to happen as a natural result of living in the Love Center for a while. When you're in the

Love Center, your energy flows into loving and serving the world. **You love people not because they deserve it, or need it—but just because they're there.** When you radiate love fairly continously, the people around you will get in touch with that part of them which is loving—and this feels really good to them. You become their access or connection to the love programming within themselves! So instead of viewing you as an "other," they begin to view you as "us." ("US" coincidentally happens to be an abbreviation for "unified-self"!) They begin to return to you the love you've helped them get in touch with. Gradually you find yourself surrounded by loving and caring people.

Thus, as a result of creating unconditional love within yourself, **you create a world of loving energy around you.** Your cooperativeness, your helpful suggestions, your giving selflessly, your honesty, your surrender of separate-self addictions, your sharing, your openness, your trust and your deeper and deeper feelings of love **are mirrored back to you by the people around you.** You live in a generous, cooperative world that you have created by your loving energy. This is the experience of the Cornucopia Center.

A part of the cornucopia that life offers is the opportunity to recognize your addictions and learn to deal with them skillfully. You will begin to appreciate that both you and the universe are unbelievably effective in setting up life situations to help you work on your addictions. Usually we ignore these situations and instead try to change the people or situations around us. As we attune more deeply to the Cornucopia Center, we "welcome the opportunity," as suggested by the Third Pathway, that life is offering us for our growth.

People who experience the Cornucopia Center remind us with cosmic humor that you've got to be very careful about what you want—because you just might get it. Life is experienced as a "cornucopia" or "horn of plenty" with an overflowing plentifulness that comes to you without straining on your part. You can usually "let things happen"

157

instead of forcing things to happen. You may need to ask for what you want, or to put energy into getting your preferences, but you increasingly experience that the world is really set up to give you everything you need—and a lot of what you preferentially desire. And this frees even more of your energy from any tendency to create the separate-self and meet its supposed needs. The flow of thoughts generated by the addictions that create your separate-self is gradually drying up. You are increasingly creating a very real experience of the "magic" world of the unified-self.

THE CONSCIOUS-AWARENESS CENTER

To review briefly, the Security, Sensation, Power, Love and Cornucopia Centers describe ways of motivating yourself. They are functional filters for shaping your experience of life. When using the first three, and even the Fourth and Fifth Centers, you may create the experience that there is something to lose and something to win in the drama of your life.

The Sixth Center in the Living Love Way, the Conscious-awareness Center, differs from the preceding centers. The first five Centers help you look at the flow of life events from a specific point of view. Suppose you've just met someone. The Security Center checks out whether s/he threatens you or makes you more secure. The Sensation Center checks out sensory possibilities, the Power Center makes you aware of how s/he affects the competitive areas your mind defends, the Love Center produces an accepting, loving perception of this new friend, and the Cornucopia Center helps you experience this person as a part of the richness of the world you live in. However, when you use the Conscious-awareness Center, your mind does not create any specific interpretation or significance of this person from a goal-oriented point of view. The goal of this Center is to view things without a goal!

The Sixth Center is thus a **method** of selfless observation—as opposed to emphasizing a goal-oriented **content.** When your mind is functioning in the Conscious-awareness Center, you are purely and simply alert to significant stimuli from both within your own body and outside your body. You avoid being reactive in the sense of imposing judgments, self-conscious classification systems, "me-vs.-them" categories, approvals or criticisms on the flow of phenomena which is happening on the screen of your consciousness. Instead the mind becomes totally receptive. It simply acts as an impartial, judgment-free observer of the passing scene—a detached witness. Like watching a movie, your mind may be enjoying—but not personally involved!

Our minds often remain in the Conscious-awareness Center for minutes or hours when we are in a movie theater. The house is darkened so that our full attention is on the screen. Unless the motion picture happens to trigger one of our addictions, we just receptively watch what is happening in a nonreactive way. We usually don't respond to what's happening by saying, "He's a good guy," or "Look what a terrible thing she did." We just let it all come in. We're receptive—not reactive. We let ourselves enjoy being passive observers who simply tune-in to the melodrama in front of us. The second we self-consciously identify with the melodrama by categorizing or judging what's happening, our consciousness leaves the Conscious-awareness Center and is functioning in a different mode.

It's interesting to note that we can actually enjoy the entire spectrum of human life when our minds watch it through the Conscious-awareness Center. Not only can we appreciate and enjoy the pleasure of the characters on the screen, but we can also let ourselves be equally enraptured by a tragic struggle or even a death scene! If these were to happen in our own lives, we would identify with the roles we are playing—and we would usually trigger separating emotions that would block our enjoyment.

159

The Sixth Center helps us see the soap opera we are creating with perspective. It helps us do what we do without identifying with it or emotionally buying into our own drama. Since the Sixth Center is a methodological center (rather than a center with a specific content), it is possible to use this center at any time. You may be operating your Conscious-awareness Center all the time—just noticing what's happening—regardless of what emotional experience or soap opera you are running. It's just a matter of tuning-in to it. This functioning of the mind can be perfected by practice. Some people seem to have a natural skill in operating their minds in this mode.

You may become proficient in the Sixth Center while you are still running heavy addictions. The experience of the Sixth Center can help you handle your addictions. You can be creating a soap opera in any of the preceding five Centers—and at the same time use the Conscious-awareness Center to watch your own soap opera on the TV screen of your consciousness!

The use of the mind in the Conscious-awareness Center helps you to develop a nonjudgmental awareness of "what is." It helps you develop **an ability to see things realistically instead of through the biases of the separate-self**—to see things from a wide panoramic perspective. It helps the mind find that subtle point of equanimity and wisdom that lies behind the up-and-down vicissitudes of the melodrama of life.

THE COSMIC CONSCIOUSNESS CENTER

To the best of our understanding, the Cosmic Consciousness Center represents the highest functioning of the human mind. Individuals who can operate their minds in this Center are extremely rare. But then, the highest levels of skill are always rare—for example, composers with the skills of Bach, Beethoven or Brahms are few and far between.

Eleventh Pathway: I am constantly aware of which of the Seven Centers of Consciousness
I am using, and I feel my energy, perceptiveness, love and inner peace
growing as I open all of the Centers of Consciousness.

In this center the mind functions almost without limits. Since it is through with resisting, clinging and ignoring, it perceives and acts in each life situation with a wisdom that most of us are fortunate to find even in hindsight. Addictive demands that create the separate-self are phantoms of the past. One lives without separateness with unconditional love and compassion for all of us and our human predicament. The mind is simultaneously and continuously functioning in terms of the seven mental factors described in Chapter 12.

In the Seventh Center of Consciousness, the mind no longer identifies with—or flows energy to activate—the separate-self "me-vs.-the world" processing of data. The mind also goes beyond love into "oneness." Although love is a beautiful experience, it has certain elements of separateness—of subject and object. While the statement "I love you" involves an enormous evolution from the "me-vs.-you" consciousness of the jungle, it still contains overtones of separateness. When the mind functions through Cosmic Consciousness programming, it goes beyond "I love you" to knowing "I am you." To experience "I love you," many boundaries of the separate-self must be eliminated. To know "I am you," all of the limitations of the separate-self must be inoperative.

Let's keep a perspective on this. A mind that can fairly continuously operate in the Love Center or Cornucopia Center **will produce a rich experience of enjoyment and happiness in life**—and the predominant energy flow will be toward loving and serving the world. **We do not need to use the pinnacle of Cosmic Consciousness to create an ideal that can make us dissatisfied with our own lives in any way.**

I feel that it is interesting for us to know about this highest level of skill in operating the mind in a way that addictively demands nothing, sees compassionately and loves totally. But it would not be realistic to lead you to

161

believe that you can expect to wholly attain it. As I see it, if we wish to enjoy our lives, we have no choice but to work on ourselves to go beyond the motivations of the Security, Sensation and Power Centers. And fortunately, it is totally practical for us to work on ourselves to predominantly live in the Love, Cornucopia and Conscious-awareness Centers. This pays off handsomely. I enjoy my life, and generally hang out in these Centers with an occasional dip into the Power Center. I don't live in the Seventh Center. So let's be realistic—and gentle with ourselves.

To make the great transition into the Cosmic Consciousness Center requires a relatively nonaddictive nurturing during infancy and childhood that limits the development of the separate-self. It may also require a continuity of dedication and practice. And there are no shortcuts; no one can do it for you or to you. But if we can make it to the Love Center, and immerse our children in this consciousness, a few of us may see our children or grandchildren approach this realization of the highest consciousness.

THE UNITIVE CONSCIOUSNESS

Cosmic Consciousness is thus seen to be a unitive awareness. One does not experience cars, trees or even rocks as separate from oneself. They are just "us." Intellectually, one is fully aware of the physical separateness, but one's **emotional perceptions** of what is self and not-self are no longer distinct or important. Most people have quick glimpses of this mode of consciousness. Once we understand about the potential of our minds for operating in this way, we can encourage and value even a few moments when our minds may spontaneously give us a peek into the beautiful world of Cosmic Consciousness.

The brief flashes of Cosmic Consciousness that some of us have now and then are characterized by knowing unity rather than separateness. You may have a feeling of being deeply centered in the middle of the universe. You may see people and things around you with a cause-and-effect insight into the ways they unfold together, interact together and evolve together. You may feel you have an incredible potential for creating whatever you may wish to create. You may be deeply tuned-in to life in a way that represents a new dimension of harmony and oneness that goes beyond any of the preceding Centers. And then the curtain of the separate-self drops again and the unitive knowing disappears from your screen of consciousness as ego gets busy again protecting or enhancing its territories.

FOUR PRICELESS GEMS

The Eleventh Pathway suggests that we maintain an awareness of which of the Seven Centers of Consciousness we are using. This can be either a foreground awareness or a background awareness. It then goes on to detail four valuable experiences that will increase each time we uplevel our Centers of Consciousness. The Eleventh Pathway promises us an increase in "energy, perceptiveness, love and inner peace" as we step by step go from one center to another.

If we look at these four benefits clearly, we realize that these are really what we are after in our lives. For most of our lives we've tried to find these four illusive yet deeply satisfying experiences by constantly arranging and rearranging the soap opera around us. **Now we're discovering that these are ultimately created by the ways in which we operate our minds.** By increasing our skills in withdrawing energy from the separate-self, and thus flowing increased energy through the unified-self, we can be more effective in creating an enjoyable life.

OPENING ALL OF THE CENTERS

The last part of the Eleventh Pathway refers to opening "all of the Centers of Consciousness." At an advanced point in our growth, the mind can go beyond polarizing into concepts of "lower" and "higher" centers with implications of "worse" and "better."

It's all here all the time—"what is" in your life, what you say and do in response to it, and the internal experience that you create of your life. The Center you're using is determined by what your mind is focusing on. It's like being in a busy city where everything is happening all the time around you—but with your perception concentrating on only a part of it. That part is set up by the filtering mind circuitry we call your Center of Consciousness.

The unified-self is totally at home with security, sensation and power—and these aspects of life are quite simple when addictive demands are absent. One has an awareness of the security aspects of living in the world—but is always willing to emotionally accept "what is" in one's life. The unified-self is also aware of sensation aspects, including food and sex, and may choose to enjoy both without creating separateness. They're just a part of the cornucopia that life offers us. The unified-self may use power in a selfless way that with perspective is seen as a higher level of loving and serving. When addictive security, sensation and power **are no longer centralized motivations of the mind,** you can open all of the centers in a way that lets you **love it all.**

Always be cautious about diagnosing the center of consciousness of others. One's clarity in perceiving the unified-self centers is especially subject to distortion. If you predominantly use the Power Center of Consciousness, you will tend to interpret people's actions in terms of power, pride, prestige and "me-vs.-them" one-upmanship. You may totally misinterpret the material-plane actions of someone whose predominant center of consciousness is the Love Center. Similarly distorting projections can occur in the mind that perceives the world primarily through the Security or Sensation Center.

The Eleventh Pathway may be viewed as another important tool to help us get in touch with our deeper intuitive wisdom. As we grow in consciousness, it acts as a tuning fork that can continually awaken that which we "know"— but do not yet functionally use in our everyday lives. When integrated with the other Pathways, the Eleventh Pathway can help us switch from the less comfortable and effective separate-self programmings of the mind into the more satisfying unified-self functionings of our remarkable biocomputers.

I am perceiving everyone, including myself, as an awakening being who is here to claim his or her birthright to the higher consciousness planes of unconditional love and oneness.

15

our journey of awakening

ALL OF US ARE A PART OF A transmission chain of hereditary genes and cultural learnings that stretches back millions of years into the past. Beginning as microscopic organisms that came together in the proper proportions of amino acids in some primordial slime, step by step we've evolved through aquatic, amphibian and land-based stages to the complex organisms we are today. Similarly, our cultural inheritance evolved bit by bit, tool by tool, idea by idea, to the rich cultural environments of today.

When we see our genetic growth and cultural accumulation in perspective, we can feel good about ourselves in our long journey from the oceans of antiquity. As we look at life around us (did you catch the 11-o'clock news?), we are constantly reminded of our unfinished work in going beyond the separate-self use of our minds to produce a cooperative unified-self energy flow—both individually and collectively.

The next step in our cultural growth lies in seeing that the problems of war, politics, economics, capital, labor, production and distribution of goods and services, and the tender, loving care of our environment **can only be solved as we make the transition from the consciousness of the separate-self to the consciousness of the unified-self.** As long as we fight like animals over a supposedly limited pie, we will continue to create conflict, animosity and violence. As we increasingly flow our energy into loving and serving each other in a selfless manner, we will find that all political and social problems have obvious solutions that will be intuitively discovered and energized. Thus turmoil may be seen as created by our addictive demands. It is a part of our long journey of awakening. The Living Love Way can help us speed up our painful evolution from separateness to the unity of cooperating brothers and sisters.

THE PLANETARY PROCESS

The Twelfth Pathway would have us perceive "everyone, including myself, as an awakening being." But how can we view everyone as an awakening being when most people are unaware of, or resistant to, consciousness growth? Everyone is continually being offered "lessons" through moment-to-moment life experiences that one's addictive demands are causing alienation and separateness. Our lives are giving us these "teachings" even though they may not be heard or understood. An early part of the process of awakening is to create enough turmoil and unhappiness (which we're doing very well, thank you) to gradually

167

open ourselves to more effective ways of operating our minds and our lives.

There's no doubt that four billion of us on the planet today are creating enough separateness, alienation and unhappiness to prepare us for more rapid growth! The real breakthrough occurs when we become willing to face the separateness, unhappiness and suffering that exist in our personal lives. That alone opens the way for us to achieve the insight that our separate-self modes of behavior simply will not work to produce happiness. When we see that we're scripting a lousy melodrama, we will find more skillful ways to create our soap opera on planet Earth.

Notice that the Twelfth Pathway does not state that we are awakened beings. Let's face it. We are not awake—but we are in the process of awakening. If you were awake, you would probably not be reading this book; if you were not on the journey of awakening, however, you would not be reading this book, either. When we talk about ourselves as awakening, this refers to our overall progress in upleveling addictions to preferences. It is also helpful to look at our work on each of our individual addictions in terms of awakening.

THREE PHASES OF GROWTH

There are three phases by which we can classify the status of an addiction as it evolves into a preference. (They are not to be confused with the three strengths of addictions—acting out, emoting out and thinking out—that we discussed in Chapter 10.) They are: the unconscious phase, the awakening phase and the conscious phase.

In the **unconscious phase,** you run your addictive tape without being aware that you are doing so, and indeed without even knowing that you have an addictive tape to run. For example, you can blame your friend for "making you angry" by not returning a vacuum cleaner you had loaned.

You unconsciously pinpoint the soap opera as the key to your problems—not your addictive programming.

In the **awakening phase,** you can energize an addictive tape—which could even have a full display of fear, anger, jealousy or whatever. And at the same time you are fully aware that you are running an addictive tape. You understand that your addictive demand in your own head is responsible for creating your emotional experience, and that it is futile to blame your "misery" on the outside world. In this stage, on one hand you will be pushing your anger button when your friend doesn't return the vacuum cleaner —but on the other hand you will also see clearly that it is your addictive demand that is the immediate, practical cause of your anger.

In the section "Handling Your Addictions" in Chapter 8, we described the three practical steps that technically define this inner work in the Living Love system. When you are doing these three specific things with one of your addictive demands, you may be sure that **you are in the awakening phase with this particular addiction.**

In the **conscious or awakened phase,** you have upleveled this addiction to a preference. The world can no longer trigger this addictive tape. You are not vulnerable to creating a separating emotional experience in this type of situation. In the conscious phase you look at "what is," and you experience a preference that your friend return the vacuum cleaner by the time you want to use it. As a preference you don't have to like being without your vacuum cleaner and you can ask your friend to return it. If you have thoroughly done your inner work and it is genuinely a preference, your love for your friend will not flicker. You will not feel emotionally separate, whether or not the vacuum cleaner is promptly returned. You can lovingly and compassionately see it all from the perspective of "us" on the long journey of awakening—instead of staying stuck in the separating illusions.

THE AWAKENED STATE

To be awake means acting consciously in the melodrama of life. You intuitively do the optimal thing in playing the game of life. Being awake also means that behind the melodrama of your life, you have a panoramic perspective born of the intuitive love and wisdom within you. It means that although you accept the responsibility for taking care of yourself, you also know that the present and the future of all of us and our children are inextricably interwoven with the welfare and health (both mental and physical) of all other beings on earth.

You're not as separate and independent as your separate-self would have you believe. Your life is deeply affected by the thoughts and actions of people halfway around the globe—as well as next door to you. We're all in the same boat.

When you are awake, the line between self and others becomes transparent. **You have the vision of living in a world of evolving people who someday will not keep themselves in constant conflict.** You have learned to use your mind in ways that enable you to feel, think, say and do cooperative, loving and serving things. You can go beyond the jungle consciousness of "I want what I can get. To heck with everybody else. I have to protect No. 1."

As you awaken, you will feel a shield of protection that will be around you at all times as your energy begins to flow through the unified-self. This means that loving is more protective than rational-minding—although with increasing consciousness we do not have to rely only on one or the other. To live surrounded by loving people who view you as "us" instead of "them" is far more protective than all of the burglar alarms, pistols, guns or nuclear bombs. Real security and safety are not achieved through living out the paranoia of the separate-self. Only the unified-self with its loving, cooperative ways can really offer us the finest possible shield of protection. And only the consciousness of the unified-self can enable us to create an experience of life that is deeply and continually satisfying.

COMPASSION AND GENTLENESS

In everyday life, "perceiving everyone, including myself, as an awakening being" means to be compassionate and gentle. It means that life is a matter of emotionally accepting where we are now **because that's where we are. It's** what is. Instead of being critical, judgmental and cynical with ourselves, we can be compassionate and understanding of how the growth process works in us. It is usually a zigzag rather than a big jump forward. We proceed by remembering and forgetting, and remembering and forgetting, and then remembering and forgetting some more.

The game is not to permit the consciousness of the separate-self to make us feel bad when we stumble. Instead we use the consciousness of the unified-self to welcome the stumbling as a part of the growth process and then to get up when we do stumble, and learn the lesson that life is offering (Third Pathway). And if we don't learn it the first time or the second time, we realize that it's O.K. to stumble until we do learn. It is inevitable that we will make mistake after mistake as we learn the skills of life.

Sometimes we use our lack of skill or our "mistakes" to become self-critical and self-conscious. We are learning that it only perpetuates the addictive demands of the separate-self when we let our minds do a hatchet job on us that continually makes us feel unworthy, hopeless and helpless. As awakening beings, we can learn to honor and "love it all." **We do not have to emotionally buy into the models of perfection that our rational minds project for us.** We can be realistic—**and accept and love ourselves and others just as we are—or as we are not.** We can realize that everyone else is on the journey to higher consciousness, too—some crawling slowly and others jogging along. We all have to make mistakes, experience hard knocks, forget and remember—and it's all a part of the journey.

From a panoramic point of view, what we call "detours" are simply **a part of the road to get from where we are to the consciousness of love and oneness.** Suppose we want to travel from San Francisco to New York. On the map it's a clear journey along I-80. But someone in an airplane could notice that because of heavy snow, there is a detour for many miles in Wyoming. **For one with a panoramic view, the detour is seen as just a part of the trip.** But our minds may make us impatient and angry, for they have addictive models of how the road should be. And that's how unhappiness begins.

As we view ourselves and others as awakening beings, we realize that everyone and everything is a process. However it may seem to the contrary, we are not rock-like or unchangeable. Given love, understanding and the proper circumstances, people really can change. No one is hopeless—including ourselves. No matter how addicted we may be today, it is always possible to change. We must work on our own heads in order to create more and more love in our lives. For love opens our hearts and helps us find the courage to let go of our addictive programming. And as we keep pointing out, it is only by decreasing our addictions and increasing our love that we can enter into the promised land of the "higher consciousness planes of unconditional love and oneness."

OUR BIRTHRIGHT

The second part of the Twelfth Pathway states that we are here to claim our birthright. And what is this birthright? It is our entitlement as human beings to create and live in the "higher consciousness planes of unconditional love and oneness." And why may these be viewed as our birthright?

The experience of love and oneness is "discovered" within each of us as **a natural state** created by the human mind when it is freed from its jungle programming. It's not that we have to learn to create love and oneness. It's that we have to stop doing what prevents us from activating this **natural tendency of human beings to love each other.**

It's as though the light of love and oneness was always turned on within us, but we've managed to cover it up so that not much of it gets through. Our birthright is a jewel that we've always had. But we are so busy living out the roles of personality about who we think we are that **we cannot discover the beautiful beings that we really are. And so here we are complaining of poverty and not having enough—when all we need to do is to claim the great birthright that we already have.**

A MORE SENSITIVE SCALE OF VALUES

We may find it helpful to have a more sensitive value scale as a moment-to-moment guide toward love and oneness. Let's imagine that we replace all knowledge of ethical

CONSCIOUSNESS VALUE SCALE

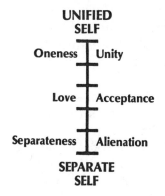

UNIFIED
SELF

Oneness | Unity

Love | Acceptance

Separateness | Alienation

SEPARATE
SELF

or moral forms, such as honesty or dishonesty, helpfulness or non-helpfulness, killing or non-killing, with a single, simple value scale. At the bottom of the scale are those

173

thoughts and acts that increase our fragmentation, separation, alienation and duality which are always generated by our separate-self programmings. At the top of the scale will be those thoughts and actions that automatically take place when we run our unified-self tapes.

Notice that this scale applies to your tapes—not the tapes of others. Suppose your boss is running an addiction and is angry with you. S/he is stuck in creating an experience of separateness and alienation toward you. It would be a misuse of this scale to use it in judging your boss. Instead, check yourself out. Are **you** experiencing separateness and alienation when your boss blames you? Can **you** accept and love your boss even when s/he's not accepting and loving you? The conscious game is for **you** to hang out at the middle or top of the value scale even when (or especially when) you perceive that people around you are running separate-self tapes.

You will discover that this is an extremely sensitive scale of ethical and moral values. It is more sensitive than the ordinary list of thou shalts and thou shalt nots that is needed for people to avoid hurting each other when their consciousness is largely motivated by the jungle centers. However, as long as people are living out their security, sensation and power addictions, the codified prescriptions of thou shalt not lie, thou shalt not steal, thou shalt not kill, etc., are useful to us as individuals, and as a society, to keep from tearing each other apart.

As we grow into higher consciousness, these form-bound moral commandments are not as helpful as the more sensitive value scale that we are discussing. That is because whatever is helpful in the codes of morality will automatically be a part of the guidance of the consciousness value scale. For example, when you steal, if you look within yourself, you see that you are living out your separate-self programming—which places you at the bottom of the scale.

If you live in a consciousness of love, there would be no one to steal from. You can only steal from "them"—and your mind no longer creates "them"—it just creates "us." When the barriers of separateness are no longer being maintained by your mind, you cannot feel deficient enough or separate enough to steal from any human being. Only the security, sensation and power demands of the separate-self could ever cause an act of theft. And when you are in the Love Center, you are beyond these separating actions.

This new value scale is a part of our birthright into "the higher consciousness planes of unconditional love and oneness." It represents a significant moral evolution. The commandments, ethical imperatives or rules that are so needed to take the rougher edge off of our jungle-type security, sensation and power addictions are experienced as outer-imposed—and our wars and our prisons attest to their limitations in producing a cooperative society.

Rules or commandments are not felt to be a part of one-self. It's like, "Here is society, and here are the things that good people do not do. I don't want to be thought of as a bad person, so I'd better follow these rules or at least look like I'm following them." Rules of conduct are thus viewed as something "they" are forcing on "us." People often follow the letter of the rule—instead of the spirit.

The rule-type moral scale often leads to guilty or self-rejecting feelings. The value scale we're describing here as a part of our awakening does not come from an outer-imposed space. Neither does it come from an inner-imposed space. For in its highest form, it is not something we do even to look good to ourselves. Instead, as we train our minds to go beyond the jungle consciousness of the separate-self, and create our realities with the unified-self programming of the Love Center, **we naturally act in the ways of wisdom.**

For example, a person in business who is motivated by the Love Center no longer has a predatory subject-object attitude toward buying cheap and selling dear. Instead the game is now to love and serve brothers and sisters by buy-ing good quality merchandise, correctly describing it and

175

selling it at a reasonable price that will let one stay in business and make a fair living. When we treat everyone as a brother or sister whom we love and serve, we do not need to refer to outer-imposed moral commandments. Our thoughts and actions automatically go toward the higher levels of our consciousness value scale since there is no one left in our perceptual field to rip off or take advantage of. We're all brothers and sisters—one great family of "us."

This attitude of treating everyone as a brother or sister can be helpful in building a prosperous business. For people will pick up the vibe that your business is run from a motivation of love and service. They will trust you and want to buy things from you.

LOVE AND ONENESS

It was pointed out in our discussion of the Eleventh Pathway that love still involves a thin degree of subject-object. There is you—and there is the person you love. There is still some separateness—however filmy. In the unitive experience, perceptive boundaries of separateness largely evaporate, and the mind can no longer continue the illusion of separateness between you and other people.

The ways in which you are like other people are so much more important than the ways in which you are not alike. In all important things in life, you know that you are just like other people—you have a human heart that feels, and you are an occasionally stumbling traveler on the long journey of learning how to create a human life filled with energy, wisdom, love, joy, happiness and purpose.

Everyone else is also on this journey. Most people will be either ahead of you or behind you in certain areas of growth—but this is not important any more. Separate-self comparisons are no longer being activated. The vista from the unified-self is beginning to enlarge the beauty and richness of your experience.

As you learn to use your mind more effectively to create a human life with increasing richness, you will find that all the stuff of life such as money, sex, relationships and "success" are still there. But they are now seen as part of the games of life, rather than as reasons for living . . . .

The purpose of life that we are now energizing has to do with learning to decrease our addictions and increase our love. The way we put it in the Living Love Way is:

The purpose of our lives is to free ourselves from all addictive traps, and thus become One with the Ocean of LIVING LOVE

PART VI

Helping It Happen

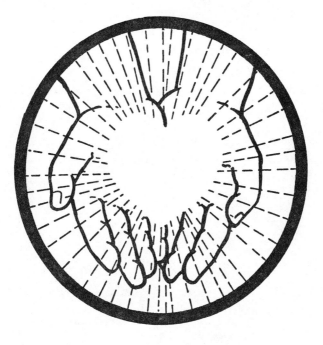

The game is to reduce your addictions and increase your love. Just wanting these to happen is about as effective as merely wanting your body to be stronger. Daily exercises or practices are needed to help your mind turn down its addictive demands and turn up its ability to love unconditionally.

16

using the pathways

THE PATHWAYS ARE TOOLS THAT can help you become the master of your mind. They help you replace automatic jungle-type programs with human programs that enable you to live your life more effectively to get the things you really want. You can never get enough of what promises real happiness—but can't deliver it: security, sensations, power, money, luxury, prestige roles to play in life, pride when you compare yourself with others, material possessions, etc. The above things **you think are it** are just unskillful culture-bound strategies to get "enough," have "enough" and be "enough." The satisfying experiences in your life that you really want are increased energy, insight and perceptiveness, tuning-in to your intuitive wisdom, loving yourself and others, joy, happiness, inner peace and a feeling that your life has purpose. Only these are deeply satisfying—and enough.

Intellectually understanding the Twelve Pathways is only a first step in helping us get what we really want in life. The second step is to resolve not to settle for a diminished life. This means a determination to work on yourself to create the enormous difference that applying the Twelve Pathways can make in your life. If you were learning to paint, your knowledge of the principles of painting and your determination to become a fine painter would only be your first steps. Then comes practice, practice and more practice. And without countless hours of practice, you will never develop the skill you need to make a "turn-around" difference in your life.

MEMORIZING THE PATHWAYS

If you are at all serious about working on yourself using the Pathways, the first step is to memorize them. Most of us have strong programming against memorizing. We hate it. We had to memorize in school, and many of us vowed never again to memorize anything. You'll have to work on yourself to overcome any addictions you may have in this area. For the Pathways cannot be used in daily practice with maximum effect unless they are deeply placed into both the conscious and unconscious parts of your mind.*

Thoroughly memorizing the Pathways so that you can **say them word perfectly when emotionally upset** is a first

*A 17" x 22" poster of the Twelve Pathways is available from Cornucopia Books, 790 Commercial Ave., Coos Bay, OR 97420 at a price of $3.00 plus $1.25 for postage and handling.

step. If you are really determined to use the Pathways as tools to improve your life, you'll be able to do it. You're doing it for you—so don't just barely memorize them so that you can haltingly reproduce them. Such an incomplete learning of the Pathways will enable your separate-self to quickly override them when you really need them in your life. When partially memorized, you may forget clauses or change words, or you won't remember to say them to yourself when you're caught up. Or you'll start to say them and get distracted before you've used them enough to give your mind the insightful clues it needs.

You don't need the Twelve Pathways when you're relaxed, clear and everything in your life is meeting your models. **You need them when you're on fire.** And that's when you'll forget them if you haven't thoroughly memorized them. One way to check yourself out is to say them clearly in front of a friend who will let you know every word you miss. For the purpose of deeply internalizing them, don't let your ego get away with missing even one word or substituting "a" for "the." Keep working until you can say them rapidly **even when you are self-conscious or upset.** Then they become real tools for your inner work.

The Living Love workbook entitled *THE METHODS WORK . . . if you do!* contains ten tips for helping you memorize the Pathways:

1. Memorize them one at a time (perhaps one a day or one a week).
2. Work with someone else.
3. Put copies around your house so that you can see and read them frequently: on the refrigerator, in the bathroom (in plastic in the shower), by the phone, etc.
4. Memorize them one word or phrase at a time: "I," "I am," "I am freeing," "I am freeing myself," etc.
5. Put them on tape and listen to them before you go to sleep, when you get up in the morning, and several

times a day.*
6. Put them to music.
7. Put them in your pocket or around your wrist.
8. Draw a picture of each Pathway.
9. Use main words as cues, "I am freeing . . . addictions."
   I am discovering . . . illusory version."
10. Read them out loud before going to sleep, upon waking in the morning and several times a day.

If you find yourself creating frustration as you memorize the Pathways, you are running addictive programming. Using the Fifth Pathway, take responsibility for creating this experience. Using the Sixth Pathway, totally accept yourself running off addictions about memorizing. Be patient and gentle with yourself—but get them memorized sooner or later.

You might find it helpful to carry a copy of the Pathways with you for a while after you have memorized them. When you are very upset, your ego can temporarily "forget" them. Looking at them will help focus your attention so that you can find the one or two that really "click." You can xerox the Pathways page at the end of Chapter 3.

THREE BASIC WAYS

We recommend three basic ways of using the Pathways as a tool for helping you turn down your addictions and turn up your love:
1. **Say all Twelve Pathways, slowly and meditatively.** When you **just do this,** you'll be using them as a tuning fork to resonate with the deeper wisdom that lies within your unconscious mind and which is not being used because of

---

*A cassette tape is available in which the Pathways are slowly and meditatively recited several times on Side 1. On Side 2, I share my poem "Our Way to Happiness." This tape can be ordered from Cornucopia Books, 790 Commercial Ave., Coos Bay, OR 97420 at the price of $6.00 plus $1.25 for postage and handling.

the runoff of your addictive programming. **Just say them as soon as possible after you become aware that you are feeling separate or upset.** Don't hesitate or stop. If you feel it would be helpful, say them two or three times or more if you are in the grip of a powerful addiction.

2. **Choose one or more of the Pathways that apply in the situation, and say them over and over.** Remember, there is no right or wrong Pathway to apply to a situation. Just pick one or more that you feel particularly open to at the time. You may wish to use a traffic counter to help you to play the game of using the Pathways. Suppose you're demanding that your landlord not raise the rent. You want to uplevel this addiction to a preference so that you can discuss this with him from a unified-self space. You might choose to work with the Third and Fourth Pathways. Try saying these Pathways one hundred times each using the counter to keep track of how you're doing. Don't think of saying the Pathways as something you "should" do, for this could give your mind a way to reject yourself if you don't complete the number you intended.

3. **Say your demand alternately with the Twelve Pathways.** This is a most effective way to use the Pathways. But to use them in this way, you will first have to formulate your addictive demand. Look carefully at what you want different at this moment from the way you are, or the way other people are, or the way life is. One way to pinpoint your addictive demand is to imagine that you have a magic genie who will give you anything you ask for. **Exactly what would you ask for right now? This is your addictive demand. Be specific—don't generalize.**

Formulate your demand in this way:

"I choose to create the experience of (insert separating emotions) because I choose to addictively demand (insert what you're addictively wanting)."

To use the Pathways in the third way, say your addictive demand and alternate with each of the Twelve Pathways.

For example:

"I choose to create the experience of irritation and frustration because I choose to addictively demand that Bob not have forgotten to buy the tickets."

"I am freeing myself from security, sensation and power addictions that make me try to forcefully control situations in my life, and thus destroy my serenity and keep me from loving myself and others."

"I choose to create the experience of irritation and frustration because I choose to addictively demand that Bob not have forgotten to buy the tickets."

"I am discovering how my consciousness-dominating addictions create my illusory version of the changing world of people and situations around me."

"I choose to create the experience of irritation and frustration because I choose to addictively demand that Bob not have forgotten to buy the tickets."

"I welcome the opportunity (even if painful) that my minute-to-minute experience offers me to become aware of the addictions I must reprogram to be liberated from my robot-like emotional patterns."

Continue in the above pattern until you have finished all Twelve Pathways. Then look at the experience you are creating. If you're still making yourself feel upset, repeat the process again one or two times—or more. A variation is to say your addictive demand alternately with one or more Pathways that especially apply to your specific demand.*

TIPS FOR WORKING ON YOURSELF

When you're caught up with an addictive demand, every minute that you spend using the Pathways in the above

*It is strongly recommended that you study the section on pinpointing addictive demands in THE METHODS WORK . . . if you do! Available from Cornucopia Books, 790 Commercial Ave., Coos Bay, OR 97420 for $4.50 plus $1.25 for postage and handling.

three ways brings you one tiny step nearer to becoming the master of your mind and your experience. Even if it is not evident at the time, you are creating a foundation for growth—a growth that is solid and valuable. The Pathways are totally portable. Once you've memorized them they will always be with you. You can use them any time, anywhere.

If you find yourself impatient and demanding results quicker than you're getting them, **work on that as an addictive demand.** You can use the Pathways in the way described above:

> "I choose to create the experience of impatience and disappointment because I choose to addictively demand that the Twelve Pathways work faster than they are working."

> "I am freeing myself from security, sensation and power addictions that make me try to forcefully control situations in my life, and thus destroy my serenity and keep me from loving myself and others."

> "I choose to create the experience of impatience and disappointment because I choose to addictively demand that the Twelve Pathways work faster than they are working."

—AND KEEP DOING IT.

Don't expect the Pathways to instantly transform your experience from anger or worry to insight and love. **You cannot use addictive programming for many decades in your life, and then say the Pathways a few times and expect this addictive programming to evaporate.** The Pathways may quickly affect some addictive programs that your ego tends to hold lightly. But on "biggies" involving relationships, sex, money, pride, prestige, control and self-rejection, you'll find that months of inner work may be needed to learn **to handle** them. Perhaps years may be needed to gradually file down some addictions so that you can uplevel them to preferences. **Or it can happen in a flash of insight!**

Put your attention on what the Pathways are pointing toward—not on trying to make your separating emotions go away. Work on the cause (your addictions) and not the symptoms (your separating emotions). Just keep saying the Pathways—perhaps as long as you are feeling upset. Keep tuned-in to small wins—appreciate and enjoy them. Using the Pathways is simple—but not easy. **But then living out your addictions for the rest of your life is even harder.**

ADDICTIVE SNARLS

We make ourselves most upset when there are several things we are simultaneously demanding. These mental sets are called "addictive snarls." The mind may have up to one or two dozen **mutually supporting** addictive demands. Upleveling only one addiction in a snarl may make little difference, for the mind has crystallized into a rock-like solidity in this particular area. It's a tough thing to overcome and may take years.

To work on an addictive snarl, first write out all of your addictive demands—and see them as a whole. See how they support each other and give a tenacious quality to the entire addictive area. Then pick the strongest demand in your life right now and work on it using the Pathways. In other words, divide and conquer. Work on one demand at a time, but keep going down the list you've made, working on your addictive demands one by one.

Knocking out the addictions that support an addictive snarl is like trying to collapse a table supported by one or two dozen legs. The table will still stand after you saw off a leg or two. But keep working on the addictions whenever your life gives you the opportunity. You weren't born with the snarl; you unknowingly programmed it in; and with patience and skill you can handle it.

Don't develop a model in your mind that consciousness growth can always be done in a few seconds or minutes.

If you have a lot of interlocking demands, you may wish to spend your entire month working on an addictive snarl that is creating unhappiness in your life. You can learn to do this in the middle of your daily activities. Be sure to ask yourself if you really want to uplevel an addiction to a preference. Or do you just want to shape up the people around you? Do you only want to stop feeling fear, frustration and anger? Remember that your addictive demand is the cause and your separating emotion is the effect. Is your mind trying to get rid of the effect without handling the cause? It can do this, of course, by suppressing your emotions—but this just sweeps the dirt under the rug and you'll have to live with the lumps. So look again at whether you're ready to handle your addiction.

Your mind will not uplevel an addiction to a preference if you don't honestly want to let go of the addiction. You can't fool your mind. You've got to really want to let go— not just **want to want** to let go. You must want to drop the addiction for yourself—not just to look good to others, or even to meet your own "should" models.

What if you want to hold on to an addictive demand even if you know it is causing you separateness and unhappiness? That's O.K. Do it. You'll have to keep running the addiction with its anger, fear, jealousy, etc. But run it consciously. That is, in the midst of your unhappiness, just keep on noticing that it is your addictive demand that is causing you to feel that way. If possible, break through the illusion that the outside world is creating your experience. This would be a good time to reread Chapters 2 and 3.

Your mind will become your friend and help you change your programming when you are broadly aware that your addictive demand is the immediate, practical cause of unhappiness—and you're ready to do something about it. Your progress with each addiction will begin when your mind has the insight that it's the addiction that's the problem, and **you're fully determined to handle your addiction.**

When you let go of an addiction, **you're not letting go of any thing worth having. You're just letting go of the basic cause of your unhappiness.** Your addictions usually involve things you think you have or should have—they are not usually about things you really have. If you really have something—and it's truly yours—you probably wouldn't be in touch with an addictive demand! You're only surrendering that which makes you suffer! You're not giving up anything valuable!

DEMANDING LESS AND LOVING MORE

For most of my life, I told myself that if someone I was living with didn't do what I wanted her to do, I had to run off some sort of miffed, petulant, irritated or angry response. How else could I shape her up so I could enjoy living with her? I was trapped in my separate-self addictive runoff. I went through two marriages in this way. Then I found the Living Love techniques for loving more skillfully.

I now work from a unified-self model that is far more effective in enabling me to enjoy my life—and create the most that's gettable in a relationship. If the person I'm living with does not meet my addictive models in some way, I work on myself. **This means handling MY addictions.** I tell myself that if I just keep on loving her, and clearly, but in a non-pressuring way, put out for what I want, I'll either get it or I won't.(!) If I get it—great. If I don't, I know that I really have enough to be happy without it (Fourth Pathway). **I'm willing to settle for what life can give me when I am loving unconditionally.** I can let go of the rest.

Sometimes the person with whom I'm involved in a relationship can't give me what I want **from a loving space.** I now see that the price I pay in lost love is much too high if I have the headset, "Do it my way—or I won't love you." But love is increased by a deep level of inner honesty and communication, and clearly asking for what I want. As the residents of Cornucopia express it:

190

Ask for what you want,
Enjoy what you get,
Work on any difference.

I find that by demanding less and loving more, I do not get everything that my mind wants in a relationship. But after having tried for many years to get my relationships to work by demanding more and/or loving less, I now regard this separate-self approach as representing a low level of skill in operating my life. My experience is that I get a hundred times more enjoyment in life (and probably twice as much of what I want) when I live in the unified-self space of demanding less and loving more. So let's get to work doing it! Wanting growth, thinking about growth or comparing yourself with others will not enable you to grow. It's your working with yourself in your actual life situations that will produce this incredible transformation of yourself, your relationships with other people, and your life. This is the promise of the Twelve Pathways.

Folk wisdom advises us that a stitch in time saves nine. Since you reap what you sow, you can quickly use the Pathways to intervene in the automatic runoff of addictive security, sensation and power tapes. This may make the difference between an enjoyable, conscious, loving life of the unified-self and a separate-self life of struggle, separateness and alienation. It's a choice between creating heaven or hell in your life.

17
getting results

THE KEY TO GETTING RAPID results from the Twelve Pathways in improving your enjoyment of life lies in using them within a few seconds after you trigger an addiction. If you permit your mind to begin churning about a problem, you give it a chance to push the emotional triggers that both make your heart beat faster and start squirting adrenalin into your blood. Once your body and rational mind build up momentum, the Twelve Pathways cannot produce the rapid change in your experience that you would like them to create.

It is therefore important that you quickly begin one of the three ways (described in the previous chapter) for using the Pathways **in the moment that your addiction is triggered.** Let's look at a hypothetical situation in which an addictive stimulus is permitted to automatically run in the classical jungle fashion. In the graph we see the addictive stimulus happening at zero seconds. (See the graph entitled "Experience Without Using Pathways" on the next page.) Let's suppose at this point someone says to you, "I think you're stupid." Usually we buy into that one (by automatically reacting with anger or anxiety) unless we are very skillful at working on ourselves.

As soon as you hear these words, the limbic neurons in the interior of the brain will activate other neurons that (1) make your body feel tense, (2) trigger a faster heartbeat (with adrenalin pouring into your bloodstream), (3) create an emotional feeling of anger and (4) activate the Department of Defense in your rational mind. The rational mind will be stimulated to scheme out the best way to make that person wrong and to hurt her/him in the traditional subject-object fashion.

The rising curve on the top graph indicates the increasing intensity of physical and emotional feelings. Notice how the curve continues to increase for a number of seconds after the addictive stimulus hits the nervous system. This, of course, is only a hypothetical example. In the case of a strong addiction, bodily tension, emotional feelings and the right-wrong rational-mind game could go on for many minutes—or even years!

YOUR CHOICE

Now let's look at what can happen when you choose to rapidly use the Twelve Pathways to activate the unified-self instead of the separate-self tapes. Let's assume that the same addictive stimulus hits you at zero seconds. Let's

EXPERIENCE WITHOUT USING PATHWAYS

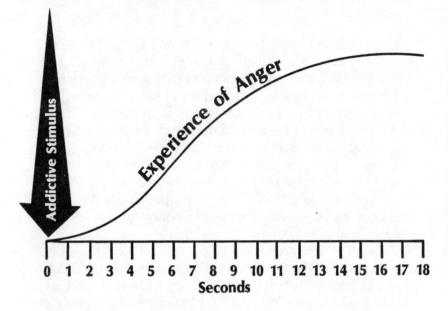

WHEN PATHWAYS ARE EFFECTIVELY USED

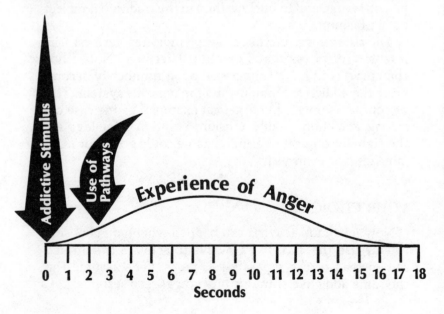

also assume that two seconds later you begin to use the Pathways as a mental tool as described in the last chapter. (See the graph entitled "When Pathways Are Effectively Used.") Notice that the emotional feelings may continue to increase for a few seconds after you begin to use the Pathways, but they may gradually begin to subside when the addictive demand tape is slowed down as the mind involves itself with the Pathways. And a big emergency "threat to survival" may not be triggered by your nervous system. The graph illustrates an example of how this can work when you have acquired a high level of skill in using the Twelve Pathways. But don't expect it to work like this the first few times you do it. It takes practice to train the mind to let go of an addictive demand.

GETTING AT THE CAUSE OF SEPARATENESS

It's important that you clearly understand the difference between suppression of the emotions and reprogramming the addictive demand. When you suppress your emotional feelings, you are inhibiting your response to an addiction by a right-wrong, good-bad program that does not work on the addiction, but instead works on muffling the emotional response.

Thus the Pathways can guide you from repression, through expression, to reprogramming the addictive demand. Then you've eliminated the cause of the problem. The mind will have no occasion to either repress or express any feelings of separateness.

It is vital to your consciousness growth that you allow yourself to feel anger, fear, frustration, jealousy, etc. In other words, the game is to turn off the addictions (the cause)—not smother the emotional expression (the effect). Hiding or not expressing your feeling of anger is like bolting down the lid on a pot of boiling water—there's going to be an explosion! It's treating symptoms and ignoring the real problem: the addiction.

By inserting your practice of the Twelve Pathways between the addictive stimulus and the automatic response of your mind, you'll have less body-mind stuff to deal with. When you first begin practicing Living Love, it may take you minutes or hours before you'll even remember about the Pathways. A strong addiction can make you buy into one situation after another—rather than seeing it consciously as part of the soap opera of your life.

Don't reject yourself when this happens—you are beautiful, lovable and capable of great inner strength. You are perfect. It's only your addictive programming that needs to be upleveled to preferential programming to enormously change your experience of your life. As you intelligently apply the Pathways month after month, you'll find that you will be able to swing into action more rapidly. And the quicker you use them, the better the results. But no matter how long it takes you in getting around to using them, it's "better late than never."

If something matters to us, we suffer sooner or later. But if nothing matters, we create boredom and the blahs. The conscious place is the fine line where we play life as a game—knowing that the nature of life is that we win some and we lose some. We play our roles in the melodrama as though our lives depended on it. But behind all that— here we are—watching it all with humorous equanimity. This frees us from unhappiness—and gives us a turned-on aliveness.

18
the transformation of your life

THE SCIENCE OF HAPPINESS IS based on the way life actually works. Happiness increases as (1) addictive demands decrease and (2) love for oneself and others increases. The more addictions you have, the less love you feel. Obviously addictions are the "germs" that play a major part in the "sickness" of the mind that we call "unhappiness."

We are in a terrible predicament. Because of our addictive demands, we're all set up to live a lifetime of unhappiness. That does not mean that we will not occasionally find pleasure. But soon thereafter, our addictive programming will make us vulnerable to creating a lot of unhappiness in our lives. It's a roller coaster—up and down.

How do we get off the roller coaster? We always create our happiness or unhappiness in life depending upon whether we use addictive or preferential programming in experiencing "what is" in our lives. This gives us the key to transforming our experience of life.

We are born with only a few addictive demands, such as for food or warmth. As we grow up, we enormously escalate our demands to cover an amazing variety of things. The "Addictive Demands" curve in the top diagram entitled "The Usual Pattern of Life" shows the expansion of our addictive programming from a low level when we are born to dizzying heights as we go through our lives. The examples of people around us ("keeping up with the Joneses") and the models offered us on the TV screen all keep feeding the seductive suggestion into the mind, "If you just had this, you would be happy." Our addictions skyrocket!

We show the addictive demand curve leveling off past middle age and slightly decreasing as one reaches old age. This just means that when you're ninety, you probably won't be addictively demanding quite as much money and sex as you demanded at age fifty! Note that the addictive demand curve usually stays very high as long as we're alive.

HOW WE CREATE DEFICIENCY

And now comes the tragedy! It lies not in either curve in itself, but in the size of the gap between the "Addictive Demands" curve and the "What Life Gives Us" curve. Please notice that the **"What Life Gives Us" curve generally remains consistently below the "Addictive Demands" curve.** Every now and then we can get life to give us something we are addictively demanding. When the "What Life Gives Us" curve then briefly meets the "Addictive Demands" curve, we create temporary happiness.

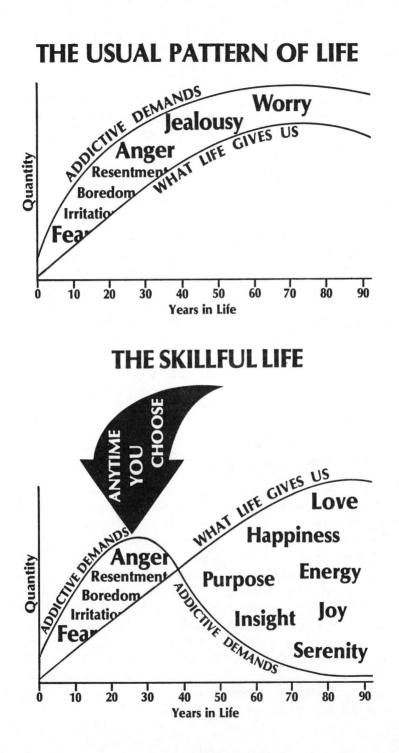

However, the operation of our minds is such that any time life gives us more, **we soon up our addictive demands.** We may tell ourselves we could be happy if we just earned $50,000 per year. Once we're earning $50,000, we now discover that we need to earn $75,000 to be happy. Our minds can only be temporarily satisfied when they run with unexamined and uncontrolled motivational systems.

We make ourselves neurotic and crazy with all of our addictive models of how life must be for us to let ourselves create the experience of serenity, love and happiness. You'll note that the gap between the "What Life Gives Us" curve and the "Addictive Demands" curve is filled with separating emotional feelings. By demanding more than life is giving us, we create an inner experience of poverty—life is not "enough." **And yet the experience of richness is only a thought away!** Over ninety-nine percent of the people on the earth are trapped in creating an unsatisfactory experience of their lives most of the time. We make ourselves far more miserable than another person ever could—even if s/he wanted to hurt us!

DEMANDING LESS—AND GETTING MORE!!!

Now let's look at what happens when you begin to use the Living Love Way as a guideline for operating your mind —and your life. Any time you choose, you can begin to work on yourself. This is one of the highest skills of human consciousness—to consciously work on the addictive demands you have programmed into your mind so as to handle them and to eventually uplevel them to preferences. In the bottom graph entitled "The Skillful Life," we've shown that this choice to work on one's inner demands took place at age twenty-five. (It could be any age except for very young children.) As one develops skill in operating one's mind, **it is possible to reduce our "Addictive Demands" well below "What Life Gives Us"** as we effectively uplevel addictions to preferences.

Now notice! A surprising thing happens to the "What Life Gives Us" curve. Our minds have warned us that if we're not addictively demanding something, the world will roll over us and we won't have "anything." But this graph shows that as we de-escalate our addictive demands, the "What Life Gives Us" curve continues to climb upward! AS WE DEMAND LESS, WE ACTUALLY BEGIN TO GET MORE FROM LIFE! You will be astounded at how your life starts flowing things to you, without intense efforting, when you are no longer addictively demanding them. By handling your addictive demands and increasing your love, you will create new energy patterns with people around you. You will begin to experience a natural flow of beautiful things into your life.

Let's discover the factors behind the surprising phenomenon shown in the graph. This happens because a decrease in your addictive demands will: first, give you more energy to put into your life, and second, increase your insight into how to apply this energy skillfully and with leverage. Third, you will stop wasting your energy on things that are not changeable and focus it on what can be changed. A fourth factor is that **you will begin to live in a field of love that you are creating.** The level of cooperation between you and the people in your life will begin to increase. And fifth, you will open yourself to experience the richness that exists in your life right now.

CREATING A LIFE OF ABUNDANCE

Looking again at the second part of the bottom diagram, you'll notice that there is still a gap between what life gives us and our addictive demand structure. **But instead of being a gap of deficiency, unhappiness and suffering, it is a space filled by experiences of richness, abundance and surplus!** When the cancerous addictions are handled, we can begin to appreciate that our lives give us far more than we need to let our minds create the experience of happiness. And the gap between the curves has now been filled with enjoyable experiences, such as love, joy, energy, perceptiveness, happiness, wisdom, insight, peace of mind and purpose in life. And now you have it. A practical method by which you can transform your entire life! This is a way in which you can work on your self-centered, emotion-backed demands that have undermined your life so subtly and persistently in the past. Now you can have the insight experience that these addictive demands are constantly undercutting what is really your birthright—a conscious, loving, satisfying life that has a deep feeling of value and purpose.

IT'S THE ONLY WORLD WE HAVE

Much of the energy of the planet today is being used in the fruitless preservation of our separate-self programming—individually, economically, socially, politically and internationally. The separating game in which each nation stockpiles weapons designed to kill people in other countries is an ultimately self-defeating attempt to find the security we would naturally have in a world of love. This incredible waste of energy could be turned into more unifying games that could help us create the great cooperative adventure of life together as loving brothers and sisters.

The jungle-flavored strategies of the separate-self can no longer help our lives to work well. Day by day, the consequences of our own separating "me-vs.-them" thoughts and feelings greatly reduce our enjoyment of life. By maximally demanding and minimally loving, we create family strife, psychosomatic illness, deception, lack of trust, money worries, blighted lives, anxiety, depression, suicide, crime, economic conflicts, ecological messes, political snarls and military disasters. We organize ourselves into both large and small power groups that further increase our contagious separateness and alienation as the battle of "us vs. them" is escalated. Most people are not even aware of the unskill-ful, self-defeating ways in which they're trying to get enough, have enough and be enough.

The future of our civilization depends on people who understand that it is to their **own individual benefit** to increase their cooperativeness, generosity and love. The transition from the separate-self to the unified-self will let us gently work toward what **we want as individuals** within a framework of understanding and insight into **our needs as a whole**—as members of groups varying in size from pair bonds of two to a global four billion. Every act of loving and caring can be an inspiration to minds that are now trapped in the vain battle for the preservation of the separate-self.

Each time you open your heart to express love for other people, without requiring their reciprocation, you are presenting a great gift to a needy world. By offering children a living model of loving more and demanding less, you can contribute a gift of supreme value to our evolving world. As you increase your ability to radiate human understanding and love to all with whom you come in contact, you can nourish their greatest hunger.

What can you do to help people realize that love is more important than anything else in creating a life filled with energy, cooperativeness, wisdom, joy, happiness and pur-pose? By working on yourself, you can take the vital first step in improving the quality of life both for yourself and others. To the degree that you acquire skill in handling your addictive demands and increasing the unconditional love in your heart for all people, your life can profoundly affect the happiness of countless people—and the genera-tions to come after us.

You are vitally needed to add to the loving energy on our planet Earth. So let's get to work. Let's start with the First Pathway:
"I am freeing myself . . . ."

APPENDIXES

appendix 1
glossary

ADDICTION: An emotion-backed demand, expectation or model that makes you upset or unhappy if it is not satisfied. It may be a demand on yourself, on another person or on a situation.

ADDICTIVE DEMAND: Another term for addiction.

ADDICTIVE SNARL: Multiple and/or conflicting emotion-backed demands. Snarls are usually supported by core beliefs or unconscious assumptions.

ADDICTIVE TAPE: Addictive programming. Words or phrases that automatically run through your mind when you are feeling separating emotions.

"BUILDING A CASE": Finding an increasing number of logic-tight reasons for making someone or something wrong and thus keeping you from emotionally accepting "what is." The crystallizing of the mind into a rock-like position that greatly limits your mental flexibility, practical give-and-take and willingness to work with a life situation.

BUYING IN: When you emotionally identify with (or emotionally reject) another person's addictive models of how s/he, someone, something or you should be, and create separating feelings in yourself.

CAUGHT UP: Upset. Feeling any separating emotions. Running addictive tapes.

CENTERED: The experience of feeling enough in yourself, and emotionally accepting other people. Things are being experienced as not threatening or constituting a problem. Feeling calm, peaceful, aware, clear-minded, not caught in an addiction. When you are centered, you are able to tune-in to your inner wisdom.

CHANGING THE "OUTSIDE WORLD": Putting energy into changing situations or people (including yourself) that you wish to be different, as contrasted with doing the inner work of upleveling your addiction to a preference.

CLEAR: Having no addictive demands triggered; feeling completely accepting; not creating any separating emotions.

CORE BELIEF: An idea, thought or belief that is deeply impressed into the conscious and unconscious functioning of your mind. Usually programmed in during childhood, a core belief is so deeply rooted that it is tenaciously held even when the intellect knows it is inaccurate. It usually persists for an entire lifetime, but with much patient practice, determination and a supporting environment, it can be altered.

EGO: The master controller of your mind that determines what is processed onto the screen of your consciousness. The ego is your friend, but it often operates from separating, addictive tapes and untrue or inappropriate core beliefs. These create the illusory experience of the separate-self whose domain of security, sensation and power is continually threatened by "what is." As you retire these separating tapes by working on your addictive programming, the ego activates tapes that let you experience the unified-self that transforms your experience of yourself and of the world around you.

EGO-MIND: A compound term usually used in referring to the joint operation of the ego (when it selects which addictions are being threatened) and the rational mind (when it searches for solutions to protect the addictions by creating "me-vs.-them," "right-wrong" and "subject-object" thought forms).

GAME: An activity of life that has dos and don'ts and a win-loss position. "Game" refers to the roles you play in life, e.g., the marriage game, the parent game, the consciousness growth game, the insurance game, the sex game, etc. When you play life as a game, you can avoid the heaviness of a "right-wrong" judgmental approach and instead create an effective and enjoyable experience of life. (This meaning of "game" should not be confused with the way in which it was used in *Games People Play* by Eric Berne, which refers to dishonest ploys that you use to manipulate another person.)

HANDLING AN ADDICTION: In the Living Love system, you are "handling an addiction" when you do all of the following three things: (1) formulate a specific demand you are running, (2) have the intellectual insight that your addictive demand is the immediate, practical cause of your experience—instead of blaming yourself, other people or external circumstances in your life and (3) work on this addiction using one of the Living Love Methods.

ILLUSION: A distorted perception of "what is." The mind produces illusions to the degree that it is running addictions.

INNER WORK: The process of consciously using the Pathways or other Living Love Methods to gain insight, uplevel your addictions to preferences, and love unconditionally.

LOVE: Emotional acceptance is both a goal of love and a means toward the goal. The experience of love is created when your perception is not being distorted by "me-vs.-them" perceptions. Love is the experience of others as "us," and not separately as "him," "her" or "them." Addictions are the enemy of love. Love increases when you handle your feelings of criticalness and separateness from yourself and others.

MELODRAMA: Your "act"; your actions on the stage of life. The purpose of this term is to help you experience the moment to moment events in your life as though they were a play or drama production—and you are an actor or actress. This helps you see your here-and-now with perspective and detachment instead of creating threatening self-conscious addictive perceptions that keep pushing your emotional buttons. Synonym: soap opera.

MODEL: An expectation. A particular form or standard of how you, someone else or a situation "should be" or "shouldn't be." Models can be either preferential or addictive.

PAYOFF: Some psychological, emotional or physical reward that can induce you to hold on to an addiction. Payoffs may be real or illusory.

PREFERENCE: A desire that cannot trigger any separating emotions or tensions in the body or mind. You have a preference if you do not create any separating emotions or thoughts when you do not get what you want. From a preferential space, you can put energy into making changes, but you are not emotionally demanding results; you remain unconditionally accepting and loving of yourself and others. Preferences help you experience life through the 4th, 5th and/or 6th Centers of Consciousness.

PROGRAMMING: The conditioning, mental sets or learnings in your mind that determine your verbal, emotional and bodily responses to life situations. Tapes in your biocomputer; mental habits. Programming may be preferential or addictive.

RATIONAL MIND: The function of your brain that analyzes, justifies and reasons. The "thinking" activity that helps you devise a strategy to get what you want in life. The rational mind is misused when you allow it to become your master and create a separating "right-wrong," "me-vs.-them" way of perceiving "what is." It serves you when it produces perceptions from the point of view of the unified-self.

RIP-OFF: A disadvantage; a way in which holding on to a demand keeps you from feeling loving, being effective and enjoying your life. Your suffering and unhappiness. Getting less than is available. Negatively affecting, e.g., "rip-off energy."

ROLLER-COASTERING: The up-and-down experience of feeling good when your addictions are satisfied and feeling afraid, frustrated, angry, etc. when life is not meeting your addictive demands. The oscillation between addictive highs and addictive lows.

SEPARATE-SELF: The illusory "me-vs.-them" perceptions that guard your security, sensation and power addictions. The mental programs that create the experience of your life as a battle against yourself, other people and/or the world, instead of the compassionate, understanding and wise flowing of energy through the unified-self that sees how everything fits into a common pattern of individual and social growth and enjoyment.

SEPARATING EMOTIONS: Feelings such as fear, disappointment, hurt, loneliness, guilt, frustration, boredom, anger and annoyance that create the illusion of alienation from yourself and/or other people.

S/HE: To be read as "she or he."

SOAP OPERA: See "melodrama." The "games" of life that are being played out on the stage of the world. The term is helpful in reminding you to see with perspective, take lightly what's happening and not get caught up in addictive seriousness.

STUFF: Your addictive demand and the consequent separating emotions (such as fear, frustration and anger) that it triggers. The chains of rationalizing, criticizing, judging and blaming thoughts and actions that are created by your addictions.

SUBJECT-OBJECT: Experiencing yourself as all-important and viewing others as pawns that help you get something you want in life—or avoid something you don't want. Subject-object refers to seeing yourself as subject and others as objects which either enhance or threaten your self-image. Not relating to people as human beings like yourself.

SUFFERING: The experience of any separating feelings in any degree. This term is used broadly in the Living Love methodology. Separateness is suffering; running unpleasant emotions is suffering; not loving yourself and others is suffering. When suffering is continual, you experience unhappiness.

TAPE: Your response to a life situation. Words that go through your mind; your conditioning; programming in your biocomputer. Tapes may be preferential or addictive.

TEACHER: People, situations or objects that put you in touch with your addictive programming. Consciousness growth requires that you open yourself to the "teachings" that occur in the daily interactions of life.

TUNE-IN TO: Become aware of; listen to; explore or experience.

"TUNNEL VISION": Viewing "what is" from a narrow perspective so that only a few elements are seen and are thus blown up in importance. Being blind to most aspects of a situation.

UNIFIED-SELF: "Us" instead of "me-vs.-them" perceptions. Programming that gives you an overall perspective of how everything fits perfectly into your journey through life, either for your growth or your enjoyment. The unified-self thus creates an experience of people and situations as a necessary or integral part of your journey—instead of the possible separate-self experience of a nuisance or threat.

"WHAT IS": Impartial, objective reality; the way the universe is unfolding as contrasted with the illusory versions you create by your self-centered addictive demands. Your perception of "what is" is thus distorted by the mind's attempt to satisfy your addictions. Often "what is" is used to remind you of what you are choosing to addictively resist, cling to or ignore (which may be real or imagined).

WISDOM: A balanced appropriate response to a life situation based on an integration of the intellect and the intuitive heart feelings.

appendix 2
where to get
living love trainings

It is possible to teach yourself to paint pictures, to operate a computer, or even to drive a car solely by reading about it and practicing all by yourself. Likewise, by carefully studying this book, the *Handbook to Higher Consciousness, A Conscious Person's Guide to Relationships* and *THE METHODS WORK.... If You Do,* it is possible to combine your study and practice so that with perseverance you can benefit from the Living Love Way in your life. Many people, however, find that it is very helpful to take the trainings we now have available. Daily contact with people who are living it and sharing it can help you clear up addictive demands that might otherwise act as stumbling blocks for a long time.

The Living Love Way emphasizes awareness, love and the joy of living. Thousands of students, housewives, laborers, businessmen, teachers, doctors, clergy and other professional people are tuning-in to the effective courses we have developed to apply the "Science of Happiness" in their everyday lives.

People who study with us are discovering that the "Science of Happiness" is completely practical—regardless of the "up-and-down" circumstances presented by the world in which we live. Once you have learned to make the Methods work effectively in your life, you will be able to devote yourself to a deeper level of inner work to heighten your enjoyment of life and to improve your interactions with people. The more advanced courses cover such topics as body and health, relationships, sexuality, conscious parenting, career, communication skills, money, relating in business, spirituality and the Methods, and defining who or what you are. Throughout all of them you will be learning to accept and love yourself more. You can come for one training—and stay for many. They all give you an opportunity to discover more about you—and allow you to grow in ways you thought would take forever.

LOCAL CENTERS

Vision Centers are small local centers around the country operated by sponsors in their homes or other convenient places. These centers are the answer for the many people who want to maintain the enthusiasm and closeness developed at a training or for anyone who is unable to attend a course at this time. Meetings are held on the first and third Tuesday evenings of each month. The highlight of each meeting is a new videotape of Ken Keyes or one of the other trainers.

You are invited to be a free guest for your first meeting. Ongoing support is offered in deepening your understanding of the skills discussed in this book. These meetings give you the opportunity to meet others who wish to grow in creativity, love, happiness and the feeling of purpose in their lives.

For a free catalog or training information, contact the Ken Keyes Center, 790 Commercial Avenue, Coos Bay, OR 97420, phone (503) 267-6412. For information on attending a Vision Center meeting, becoming a Vision Center sponsor or purchasing one of the Living Love videotapes, write or phone Vision Center Headquarters, 790 Commercial Avenue, Coos Bay, OR 97420, phone (503) 267-5683.

appendix 3
other books by ken

Handbook to Higher Consciousness
by Ken Keyes, Jr.
Perfectbound, $3.95
This is the basic text in the Living Love system. In addition
to describing the Twelve Pathways, it introduces five other
methods for working on your addictions. It has chapters on
applying these life-giving principles to different areas of
your life. Countless people have experienced that their
lives have changed dramatically from the time they began
to use the practical methods explained in the *Handbook to
Higher Consciousness*.

A Conscious Person's Guide to Relationships
by Ken Keyes, Jr.
Perfectbound, $3.95
This guide shows you how to use the techniques of Living Love to create a more delightful relationship with the person you have chosen to be with. Seven guidelines are offered for entering into a relationship. There are also seven guidelines for being in a relationship, and seven guidelines for decreasing your involvement in a relationship. It is enjoyable to read, realistic in its approach and immensely helpful if you have a relationship or wish to find one. It will show you how to gradually create the high level of love and enjoyment you've wanted to share with your partner.

How to Make Your Life Work or Why Aren't You Happy?
by Ken Keyes, Jr. and Bruce Burkan
Perfectbound, $2.95
This simple book is fun to read! Every other page is a delightful cartoon that adds meaning to the message. It can be a helpful introduction to Living Love.

Taming Your Mind
by Ken Keyes, Jr.
Clothbound, $7.95
This enjoyable book (which has been in print for 30 years) shows you how to use your mind more effectively. It contains about 80 full-page drawings by Ted Key. It is written in a deeply effective but entertaining style. It was previously published under the title *How to Develop Your Thinking Ability.* It was adopted by two book clubs and has sold over 100,000 copies.

The Hundredth Monkey
by Ken Keyes, Jr.
Pocketbook, $2.00
There is no cure for nuclear war—ONLY PREVENTION! This book points out the unacceptability of nuclear weapons

for human health. It challenges you to take a new look at your priorities. With the intriguing new concept about the power of our combined efforts, it shows how you can dispel old myths and create a new vision.

Your Heart's Desire—A Loving Relationship
by Ken Keyes, Jr.
Perfectbound, $3.95
Do you want to bring the magic of enduring love into your relationship? Without your partner having to change, shifts in your awareness can enable you to regain the wonderfully warm feelings you once had for each other. This book can dramatically help you deepen the harmony, love, trust and support you now enjoy.

Prescriptions for Happiness
by Ken Keyes, Jr.
Perfectbound, $2.00
Treat yourself to more happiness by having these prescriptions handy! This book can help you tune-in to your own self-worth, your right to an enriched life. A perfect gift to yourself or anyone else you treasure.

Available in bookstores or from Cornucopia Books, 790 Commercial Ave., Coos Bay, OR 97420. Send cash with your order, including the shipping fee of $1.25 for an order up to $9.95. Please add $1.25 for each additional $10 in the order or specify UPS collect for the shipping charges.

appendix 4
a career in loving and serving the world

Many people today see the futility, even danger, of living a totally self-centered life. They are longing for the deeper satisfactions that come from giving of themselves and their time to help our world work better. **They would like to experience that their lives really can make a difference.**

Would you be interested in a career devoted to teaching people to discover new choices in handling life situations using the Living Love techniques? Would you like to help people increase their joy of living in fundamental ways that can bring more love and happiness into their lives? Would you like to help mothers, fathers and children learn life skills that can continue to benefit untold generations in the future? Would you like, directly or indirectly, to help the four billion people on our planet to realize their common humanness as fellow voyagers on planet earth and thus play a part in reducing the probabilities of future wars?

If you find yourself saying "yes" to many of these questions, you may wish to explore the staff program of the Ken Keyes Center. By choosing this new career, you will be part of an effective group of men and women who are devoting their lives to sharing these goals. You will be living with people who care enough about their lives to eat nutritiously, exercise prudently and reduce the wear and tear of psychological stress and tension by following the principles described in this book. In this supporting environment, you will be cooperating with brothers and sisters who are transforming their lives while learning to love everyone unconditionally.

If you feel drawn to this high-energy, totally-involving life of loving and serving the world, and are free from financial or family responsibilities that would prevent you from totally devoting yourself to this career, write to me soon. I prefer that you write rather than phone. I will answer promptly. Address all letters to:

Ken Keyes, Jr.
Ken Keyes Center
790 Commercial Ave.
Coos Bay, OR 97420

Index

A

Abundance, 156-158
  creating, 201-202
Accepting emotionally, 6,
  16-18
  yourself, 35-36, 78-86
Acting out, 97-98
Addictions
  acting out, 97-98
  addicted to getting rid of,
    12, 31, 86
  bodily effects of, 192-193
  cause separating emotions,
    5
  decreased by love, 35
  definition of, 4-5, 207
  destroy enjoyment, 20, 31
  emoting out, 97-99
  experience of deficiency,
    17, 198-200

Addictions (cont.)
  food, 147-148
  handling, 72-73, 84, 138,
    160, 169, 189-190, 209
  illness, cause of, 144
  intelligence, 20
  inventory of, 72
  multiple, 32, 188-189, 207
  not bad, 19
  not serious, 31-32
  perception, 30, 38-39, 42-
    43, 45
  psychosomatic effects of,
    42, 47, 50, 144, 150
  reduce creativity, 30-31
  resisting, clinging and
    ignoring, 15-20
  rip-offs of, 29-31
  signs of, 5
  social improvement, 54-
    56, 129, 202-203

F

G

H

I